WALKING TALL IN TOUGH TIME

AN EVERYDAY GUIDE TO DEALING WITH EVERYDAY CHALLENGES...

FROM CHANNELS AWARD WINNING AUTHOR

GREAT IGWE

..WEGI PUBLISHING HOUSE. NEW YORK, MARYLAND

Walking Tall In Tough Times

© 2019 GREAT IGWE

All rights reserved. Except as permitted under The U.S Copyright Act of 1976. No part of this publication may be reproduced, distributed, or transmitted in any form or by any means, including photocopying, recording, or other electronic or mechanical methods, without the prior written permission of the publisher, except in the case of brief quotations embodied in critical reviews and certain other noncommercial uses permitted by copyright law. For permission requests, write to the publisher, addressed "Attention: Permissions Coordinator," at the address below.

Unless otherwise noted, scriptures quotations are from the holy bible, new international version (NIV), ©1973, 1978, 1984 by the international Bible Society. Used by permission of Zondervan. All rights reserved. Scriptures quotations marked (KJV) are taken from the King James Version of the Bible. Scripture quotations marked (NKJV) are taken from the New King James version, ©1979, 1980, 1982, 1984 by Thomas Nelson, Inc. used by permission. All rights reserved.

Published in Manhattan, New York by WEGI Publishing House,

WEGI Publishing House

6528 Lower Manhattan Avenue

New York, NY 10004

www.WegiGroup.com

First Published 2019

ISBN: 978-1-7332803-0-3

Library of Congress Control Number: 2019909077

Printed in the United States of America.

WEGI Publishing House is a Subsidiary of the WEGI Group, Inc. The WEGI Publishing House Name and Logo are trademarks of WEGI Group, Inc. Quantity sales. Special discounts are available on quantity purchases by corporations, associations, and others. For details, contact the publisher at the address above. *Email:* infor@wegigroup.com. *Tel;* +1 (240)-688-2092

FORWARD

For many years, I have read four to five books per week as part of my devotional study and research practices. This is a helpful habit for a public speaker and preacher. Unfortunately, I have found that if I receive only one or two fresh ideas or new insights from a book; I have done well. This means that many weeks I spend $60 - $100 for four to eight new ideas or devotional inspirations.

"Walking Tall in Tough Times", however, is an incredible treasure! Every chapter is chocked full of timely quotes, scripture references, and practical steps of action that can change any reader's life. What a valuable resource! When I started reading this book, I realized that each chapter could be read as part of a daily devotional. In fact, even the quotes from famous historic figures are worth memorizing.

Therefore, I recommend that you start off by reading this work from cover to cover. Milk it for both content and encouragement. As you do, faith and revelation will rise up in your heart. Giant killing faith will inspire you and begin to permeate your life. After your read first, I would re-read the chapters that address the greatest needs. As a diagnostic tool, it will lead you through a process of strengthening and building your faith.

Great Igwe has written a classic work that is easy to read and to digest. I recommend setting aside prayer sessions to go along with the reading. Just like working out with a trainer, getting the right diet and amount of rest, you're bound to grow strong muscles. Prepare to be lovingly challenged; prepare to be changed. Don't get side tracked until you've devoured this well written book. After finishing this work, you'll boldly sing the words to the old hymn, "We've come this far by faith".

I close this forward by stating the words to the song: We've come this far by faith!

Leaning on the Lord
Trusting in His Holy word
He's never failed me yet.
Oh' can't turn around
We've come this far by faith
Don't be discouraged when trouble comes into your life
He will bear your burdens oh
He will remove all the misery and strife
And that's why
We've come this far by faith
Leaning on the Lord
Trusting in His Holy Word
He never failed me yet
Oh' can't turn around
We've come this far by faith
Just the other day
I heard a man say
He didn't believe in God's words
But I can truly say The Lord will make a way
Because he never failed me.

Bishop Harry Jackson Jr.

Senior Pastor, Hope Christian Church

Beltsville Maryland USA

PREFACE

Out of nowhere, the storms of life hit us without warning. The loss of a loved one, a broken relationship, loss of a job and properties. A terrible accident, illness or the failure of a business. This is tough challenges that people all over the world are being confronted with daily in their respective life. We don't have the power to choose what happens to us, neither can we as humans choose the nature and severity of the problems and challenges that confronts us every day. But one thing we sure can do, and has the power to control is the way we respond to these challenges and how we fight through it. Life is like an ocean and every one of us are born sailors, sailing through this ocean. Everybody shall one day encounter a storm, be it the wealthy, the educated, the poor, the uneducated, the single or married, the sick or healthy. The storms of life is not a respecter of race, religion or country of birth, but rather the storms of life is a respecter of courage, boldness, persistent, firmness of purpose and positive attitude.

Walking tall in tough times, is a book that will certainly arm and spur you to take tough decisions and actions necessary to bring about a change in your life. It will also help you change your negative perceptions and response to the challenges you are going through and put you on a part to true success. The principles and practical steps that are outlined in this book is not based on head knowledge, but rather are founded on experiential knowledge and scriptural examples that will certainly leave you transformed. This book will undoubtedly stir you to leave your comfort zone to your rightful place of influence and power. It will forge you to become uncomfortable with mediocrity and average existence. Buckle up as I take you through this journey of self-freedom and reawakening. Happy read.

PRAISE FOR WALKING TALL IN TOUGH TIMES

Great Igwe has masterfully weaved in this book a compass for standing taller than any circumstances the journey of life may throw at you. The indwelling peace that passes understanding creates calmness and serenity in the midst of chaos and storms of this world. Faith is the vehicle that delivers your inheritance in spiritual places to the physical realm and this book shows you the training that occurs in-between both stages. This will definitely strengthen your faith!

Pastor Princeton Anyim

Lead Pastor Christ Academy

Maryland USA.

We all face life challenges but how we approach these challenges is what makes us stand out. This book hits the nail on the head in that it gives guidance on overcoming these challenges and sets you apart as you walk tall. Like its author's name, it is a Great book that will surely get you going!

Amban Anjeh,

Career Specialist,

Morgan State University. Baltimore USA

Walking tall in tough times is electrifying and transformational. From one chapter to the next takes you on a Journey of truth and freedom. It is not just another Read it is a Revolution!!!!! Bound to happen to anyone that reads it. These things are written to stir up a passion in each of our lives for the tomorrow's that hold great promise! This is a book of hope and triumph. It speaks of the more that God alone can offer.

Evangelist Keshia Freeland

Founder/ President loveaflame Intl.

"In a style somewhere between that of Myles Munroe and Joel Osteen, Great Igwe grounds a simple message of self-empowerment from biblical and personal experience... like popular preacher T.D Jakes, Great has a rare gift of reaching the weakest of men in a unique way I have never seen before. This lends authenticity to his words in this masterpiece.

Darwin Hobbs

Chief Editor, WEGI Publishing. New York

ACKNOWLEDGEMENT

This project would not have been completed without the effort of some amazing and remarkable people who have labored night and day with me to bring this idea to reality. I like to appreciate members of the editorial team Clark Neon, Wu Chang and Joy Ehonwa. Furthermore, I like to appreciate everyone at WIGE Group for the awesome job they did through the publishing of this book. I also would like to acknowledge the effort of the graphic designer Mr Makmund, my dearest friend Evangelist Keshia Freeland for her words of encouragement and support, my Pastor and mentor Bishop Harry Jackson Jr for his teachings that has impacted my life immensely. My Paddy Paddy Chidera for her words of encouragement and support. My sister from another mother Patricia Anyanwu, who from day one have never stopped being there and cheering me up to keep pushing. Lastly I like to acknowledge my mum and siblings for their love, support and prayers. May God richly bless you all?

DEDICATION

For the strength and courage you have shown, the determination never to give up despite the hurt and heartbreak. The positive attitude you have maintained, the scars you bear which tells of your boldness and battles that you have fought. I dedicate this book to you for never giving up. You are my hero!

TABLE OF CONTENT

Forward	III
Preface	V
Praise For Walking Tall In Tough Times	VII
Acknowledgement	IX
Dedication	X
Introduction	1
Chapter One There Is Success In Failure	5
Chapter Two You Can Live A Worry-Free Life	16
Chapter Three A Little Smile Can Change A Lot	25
Chapter Four Peace Amid Storms	33
Chapter Five Unsinkable Faith	47
Chapter Six Rise Up And Fight	70

Chapter Seven
Rise Up And Face Your Fear	**84**

Chapter Eight
Give Up On Giving Up	**102**

Chapter Nine
Anything Is Possible If You Believe	**120**

Chapter Ten
If They Can Do It, You Can	**129**

Chapter Eleven
You Matter	**161**

Chapter Twelve
Practical Tools For Walking Tall In Tough Times	**188**

INTRODUCTION

Challenges are part of everyday life. They make us stronger and without them, life becomes somewhat meaningless because we have nothing to compare the good times to. Facing up to challenges and living through them gives us the experiences that make up our lives. However, it's important to remember that, whatever the problem, there is almost always a solution, and an end to it. Have you ever thought how great it would be to live your life the way God intends you to? Lay aside all weight and excel in your area of calling, ministry, family and business!

Friend, you will inevitably face challenges and storms in every arena as you progress towards your destiny. Being a Christian does not exempt you from them, but they come for a good purpose. Be of good cheer and buckle up, because God has placed this book in your hands for a divine purpose; this is your time to be set free from any spiritual, social, financial or emotional bondage you are currently battling, or may confront in the future. This is your time to expand and claim your territory! Do not be a victim of the devil. Be a victor instead! Hear what God is saying.

There are spiritual tools to help you overcome the storms of life. Perhaps you have heard the saying, "Into each life some rain must fall." Well, what if what you're experiencing is more of a flood? I've observed that trials often come in numbers. People of faith know drizzles, but we also know full-blown storms.

When it is raining in my life, I like to turn to the story of Noah (Genesis 6-9:17). He knew a storm. In fact, he knew one that was so long and so strong that it virtually wiped out everything around him. Because Noah had no choice but to trust in God for his very survival, his story serves as powerful inspiration for us.

The thing that most impresses me about Noah is his faith. It's often easy to think about our faith solely as an internal anchor when we hit hard times, but that wasn't the case for Noah. His was accompanied by the building of a huge, physical ark. This external ark was illustrative of his internal life. It was a tribute to his obedience to God, the very thing that saved him. Just as Noah used everyday tools to build the ark, there are everyday spiritual tools that we can employ to successfully navigate adversity. These simple but practical tools are very rewarding if followed diligently, and will help us honor God in the midst of life's storms:

1. Stand on God's promises. Search the Bible for encouragement and promises particular to your situation and study these verses. Declare those promises aloud at least once daily, claiming them by faith. It's not a coincidence that the ark was floating on water. At times scripture is our only solid ground to stand on; it can and will keep us afloat.

2. Pray without ceasing. I Thessalonians 5:17 encourages us to pray continually. There are two ways this can play out. First, you can pray on your own to God throughout the day; an ongoing dialogue of sharing and listening to Him. God will faithfully give us specific guidance in order to save us, just as He did for Noah. Second, we can meet with one or more fellow believers to lift pressing concerns up to God in unity. Group prayer like this unleashes God's Spirit in an amazing way.

3. Affirm your faith with praise. God delights in hearing our thanksgiving and praise, whether we have traveled through the storm, or we're still going through it. Paul encourages each of us to always petition God with thanksgiving (Philippians 4:6) because he knew this principle well, having been beaten, shipwrecked, and imprisoned. Thanksgiving reminds us of the goodness of God and strengthens our faith.

4. **Keep showing up.** Great accomplishments begin and end with small steps. The massive ark was built one piece of wood at a time. Our daily faithfulness in small ways opens the door for God to do incredible things we cannot do. We must take tangible action to see changes happen.

5. **Believe in miracles.** Sometimes we hope for a miracle and it doesn't happen. But sometimes we hope for a miracle and it does. Take the limits off of God. Open the door for Him to work.

The ark was built plank by plank, nail by nail. For us, this would be prayer by prayer, affirmation by affirmation. God's presence will never leave us, so we are never without hope. He will see us through. After the rain, the sun will shine again. Note that when the storm ends, you won't be where you started. You will be changed, just as the ark took Noah to a new location to start afresh. Trust the One who works all things for our good. Keep looking up, and you will see the rainbow.

This book will equip you with the principles that God has laid down for you to fight the good fight of faith by His strength, His Word and prayer. Isaiah 40:31 discloses how God operates when His children go through storms of life, stressing the significance of total surrender to His will and providence to help us endure.

Facing tough periods is a way to push ourselves and see what we are capable of through faith. Many people make their problems their defining inheritance. It's all they think and talk about. They bring it up in every conversation and try their best to convince other people to believe and accept that they are going through a great tragedy which has rendered them helpless and so the reason for their failures in life, work, school, relationships and marriage, is their tragedy or challenges.

Countless people let their external situations get the better of them. They become slaves to their negative and depressive thoughts, and the more they validate those thoughts, the stronger they become. Soon enough, a year or three passes and the same people who were happy, healthy and productive, become depressed, tired and hopeless. Instead of seeing the things in the world around us that can be opportunities and tools which can help us in getting to a better place, we stay stuck and focused on the things which aren't pleasing and gratifying to us.

While going through failures and traumatic events in life is hard, it's important that we try to learn about our own selves through our darkest times and find hope in our ability to come out of tough times stronger, walking tall as role model of victory over life's storms. Through this book I intend to reveal to you working tools and practical wisdom that will arm you to get through and find motivation in the darkest of the days, bearing in mind that nothing lasts forever.

This book will provoke you to these tough actions:

1. To hold on until the light breaks, the tides turn, and the times change for the better; to tenaciously dig in and bloom where you are planted, maintaining a cheerful attitude while you are going through such obviously difficult situations. In the process, you will inspire others to choose the noble and positive outlook.

2. To make a bold and daring move, recognizing an era has come to an end and beginning a creative transition. This book will surely get you started on the path to success again. While you can't control the economy or the other forces of change, you can position yourself to survive and even thrive in challenging times. Don't get caught unawares.

It is my desire to use this book to arm and prepare you for when those trying times come knocking at your door, because they certainly will.

Chapter One

THERE IS SUCCESS IN FAILURE

"Lord, give me the guidance to know when to hold on and when to let go and the grace to make the right decision with boldness and dignity."

— *Robert Schuller*

This could be the most important prayer you've ever prayed. Indeed, failure is the best thing that ever happened to you. You failed; I have failed too. Some have failed in their marriage, academics, career, relationship, ministry and some in parenting. The truth is that everyone on the planet has failed at some point. Some gave up after failing the first time. You failed once and you're thinking about giving up? You are ready to join all the others and accept your fate?

It's no secret that our worst fear is often failure. But what if failure is a good thing? "Failure is success in progress," Albert Einstein once said. The great scientist was on to something. Encountering our fears and failures prompts the most necessary changes in our lives and our businesses. Here's why every person, and every business, needs to fail at some point; failure is the very seed of growth and success.

1. Failure creates extraordinary change

Failure can act as a seed for two things: a road to despair or a springboard to growth. What grows out of the initial failure is entirely up to the person who "failed." It's easy to become downtrodden and lose motivation when things don't go as planned. Instead, use the failure as a mechanism to reset your perspective, make a mental change or embark on a new, much-needed direction.

Failure is necessary to shake things up. Otherwise, we would coast along comfortably but we wouldn't make any quantum leaps.

2. Failure builds tough skin

Failure has an effect similar to a calloused heel. It's the protective layer we acquire from going around the block a few times and hitting a few bumps. Left soft and unprotected, we easily become injured. Failure builds a thick skin that can help anyone enter the big leagues without fear.

3. Failure keeps the ego in check

Remaining down to earth and honest is a challenge in today's world. When we begin to experience constant success many resort to dishonesty if it means not losing what they have. They become slaves to success and before realizing it, they'll do anything to stay on top, things they would never have imagined. Partnerships and friendships are ruined. Family conflicts abound. It's all downhill from there, maybe except for the bank account. Failure humbles us when we so desperately need to be humbled. It helps us remember where we came from and keeps us in check.

4. Failure creates "aha" moments

Failure creates the moment when something is finally seen, found or understood in a way like never before. I call it the "aha" moment. Why?

It's just like solving a complicated math problem. It's tough to understand at first, but walk away for a moment and, suddenly, something clicks. The answer just comes out of nowhere. However, it's not really coming from "nowhere." It comes from a buildup within our minds as the constricting thoughts of failure and fear expand. The expansion results in an explosive energy that breaks us out of constriction and into a highly energetic, creative state when things become clear and new insight is gained.

5. Failure propels growth in a person

Failure prepares us for what lies ahead. Almost every day, entrepreneurs come across things they didn't know they needed to know. Failures catalyze much of this knowledge because they are unexpected. How else do we learn what we don't know we need to know? It's never something that can be planned.

Failure — we all come in contact with it. And more often than not, we dread even entertaining the idea of failing. As a society, we see failure to be detrimental to our success. From childhood, we are taught to avoid failure. In school, we aim to get A's, so that we can get into a good university or get a good job offer after university. We avoid getting an 'F' like the plague because that would mean we failed at something. As a matter of fact, in the letter grading system, F is the only letter grade which corresponds to the first letter of what it stands for: failure. In this subtle way, the idea that failure is not good for us becomes embedded in our minds and we try to avoid it. Instead of seeing failure as a natural part of life, we see it as very negative.

Two world-renowned psychologists, Daniel Kahneman and Amos Tversky, won the Nobel Prize for their work, which explains why we are so averse to failure. What they found is that the effect of loss is twice as great as the gain from a win. This astounding conclusion indicates the great negative impact a loss has on us as individuals; much greater than the impact of a win. Thus, it explains why we as humans would go to great lengths to avoid loss or failure.

What is interesting is that two of the tech giants of our century, both of whom are worth billions of dollars, have a very different mindset to failure: they are tolerant of it and embrace it. Both Jack Ma and Jeff Bezos believe that it is okay to fail, and that failure is part of the process. Ma has always been very vocal about failure, and most recently, in an interview at the World Economic Forum, he recounted his failures, such as: not getting a job in KFC, when 24 people applied and 23 got it. Or not getting a job as a server in a hotel, when his cousin did. Or not being able to get into Harvard, while he applied 10 times. He explains that all these failures prepared him for his path as a CEO.

Jeff Bezos, on the other hand, emphasizes that being tolerant of failure is a big part of the culture at Amazon and is responsible for its big successes. In a piece compiled by *Business Insider*, Bezos states that if you do not innovate, then you are leaving a lot on the table. In a letter to shareholders, he said "Failure comes part and parcel with invention. It's not optional. We understand that and believe in failing early and iterating until we get it right."

What this teaches us, is that although failure can be painful and although we as people have developed an aversion to it, it actually can allow us to unlock great potential. But in order to do so, we must change our mindset on failure. Instead of seeing it as something detrimental to success, we must see it as a tool for success, a tool that helps us refine our path and allows us to learn what works and what does not. In such a way, we can see it as a normal part of the innovation of our own lives, not as something detrimental to life.

Are you committed to winning in your own life? The quickest way to tell is how you view failure. Winners view failure as the path to success. Losers view failure through the lens of a fixed mindset. But if you want to achieve and win in life you must be okay with failing. As Les Brown said, "You have to fail your way to success."

Overthinking anything is a disease. If you want to change your life in any way, you need to start acting today, not tomorrow or next week. If you want to lose weight, clear your cupboards of bad food, start exercising, and begin planning your meals and workouts for the following day. Or, if you want to start an online business, quit waiting for the right time. Act by buying your domain, creating content, and getting started. Zig Ziglar said, "You don't have to be great to start but you have to start to be great."

> *"You have to fail your way to success."*
>
> — ***Les Brown***

Success is the result of your attitude, and your attitude is a choice. Hence, success is a matter of choice and not chance. Success is never an accident. It's doing the hard work repeatedly. It's creating a vision for your life and making it happen. Success is creating a positive attitude that will let you go from one failure to the next with no lack of enthusiasm. Success is a choice; choose to believe in you!

Your positive action combined with positive thinking results in success. Action plus the right thoughts, over time, will create massive success. Too many people are lacking in one or the other and wonder why they don't achieve greatness. You need both. Without action, positive thinking will only make you feel good. Without positive thinking, it will be way too easy to give up quickly. Cultivating both will set you up to achieve your wildest dreams.

True character is doing the right thing even when no one is watching. The discipline you exercise when you are alone is your true character. If you want to achieve greatness in your life you have to keep the little promises you make to yourself, because the difference between a great man and a little man is their commitment to integrity and hard work. Hard work always wins and integrity always prevails.

Choose to be committed to achieving your goals. Once you have the right mindset and lofty goals you can become the greatest version of yourself. As long as you have your eyes on the goal, you don't see the obstacles. Focus on the goal, not the obstacles. The bigger the goal, the more obstacles you will face. But if you keep your eye on the target you will find ways around these obstacles and ultimately reach your goal.

> *"The trials of this life will ultimately lead to joy,*
>
> *If we patiently trust in God's plan*
>
> *And discover how to use adversity to grow stronger."*
>
> — ***Bishop Harry Jackson***

We all cope with failures every day, and it can be unpleasant. I'm sure you failed the first time you tried to ride a bike; some people may have even had a bad fall. They have become scared of the pain and embarrassment; they might never touch another bicycle again. But then there are others who failed again and again and again. Battered and bruised, they just wouldn't stop. What is the difference between the two? Simple; how they think and see failure. So, failure is beneficial to your future. Why would anyone see failure as beneficial? Here are the good reasons you should embrace failure.

1. You have a story to tell tomorrow

Who cares about your story? Well, tell that to the young man who started rapping in Detroit. His name was B Rabbit. The first time that he stepped on stage, he got stage fright, began stuttering and couldn't speak. He was mocked, jeered and booed off the stage.

Despite the fear and embarrassment, he never gave up. He said in one of his songs that success was his only option, and failure was not. His name is Eminem. Who cares about his failure? His father abandoned him, he was abused by his mother, and he grew up in a trailer park, but his belief in himself and his passion for music were so strong that this skinny kid from St. Joseph, Missouri, became not only the highest selling rapper of all time, but also the best-selling musician of this century!

> *"If you must succeed,*
>
> *Then embrace embarrassment*
>
> *Because it comes with the package."*
>
> — **Great Igwe**

Now there are millions of people who could recite that story in much greater detail without thinking twice. But remember this: to be successful you must be different. Failure is the best thing that ever happened to you because it gives you a great comeback story.

2. You learn

We often forget the past failures of others. Someone as successful as Oprah Winfrey must have just got lucky with wealth, right? Well, Oprah was born to a teenage mother without a dollar to her name. Not only did she have to endure tough living conditions, she was also sexually abused when she was just nine years old. At age 14 she got pregnant but being so young, her son died shortly after birth.

After this experience, Oprah went to live with her father Vernon, who encouraged her to focus on her schooling to get her life back on track. Oprah put everything into her school work, eventually earning a full scholarship at Tennessee State University where she majored in communications.

Her first job was helping a small radio station, where she observed how the industry worked. Oprah thought she finally had her big break when she was hired by a local television station to read the news, but things didn't go as planned. Oprah was fired for being "unfit for television." She later found work at another TV station. She worked many low paying jobs until she decided to relocate to Chicago, to host a station's low-rated talk show called AM Chicago. Within a few months, the show went from last in the ratings to higher than "Donahue," which was the number one show at the time.

This led to the show being renamed *The Oprah Winfrey Show*! Despite the setbacks, failures, rejections, abuse and challenges, Oprah never gave up or threw in the towel. She fought through and went on to become a household name. She is now valued at over $2.7 billion. It is motivating and appealing to talk about Oprah's prowess and to admire and desire her wealth, fame and status, but let's not forget her story; how she got here and the things she fought through.

> "Don't desire the fame if
>
> You are not ready to go through the fire."
>
> *— Sylvester Stallone*

3. You develop mental strength

I am sure developing mental strength might seem like a raw deal. I mean you must fail to get it. But it is relatively simple. You learn from your failures. Every single successful person says their failures are what drove them to become successful. What happens when you make an embarrassing mistake? Do you ever make that mistake again? Well, you'll do everything in your power not to. You have two options:

1. Fail, give up and never try again, or

2. Fail and become so possessed with not failing again that you use it as fuel to drive you forward every single day. Failure grows and builds your character. Jack Ma, founder of Alibaba, once said, "I'd rather hire an employee who has failed in his career and mastered the art of success than an employee who has never failed."

Have you read or heard of the guy Thomas Edison? He is the guy who kept on working even after the 100th failure. I'm sure like me, you've heard that many times. But what did you really take from it? The invention of the light bulb was a historical landmark. Afterwards he was interviewed, and a reporter asked him, "After failing more than 100 times, what led to your success?" His reply was incredible. He said: "Who told you I failed in those 100 attempts? In fact, I learned over 100 ways of not making a light bulb."

Wow, each time I read Mr. Edison's reply I am amazed. That's the positive mindset you can learn from Mr. Edison when you fail. Failure can make you stronger, it just depends on your mindset and approach to it.

"You may have to fight a battle more

Than once to win it."

— Margaret Thatcher

Who cares about your failures when you succeed? No one. Your failures are forgotten. I'm sure you've head of the Wright brothers who are credited with inventing the airplane, but have you heard of Samuel Pierpont Langley? I doubt you have. Well, he was the other person also attempting to build the airplane at the same time the Wright brothers were.

In fact, he had a whole lot of support. Langley had achieved some renown with the academic community as an astronomer, which earned him many high ranking and prestigious positions. He was the secretary of the Smithsonian Institution. He had been an assistant in the Harvard College Observatory and professor of mathematics at the United States Naval Academy.

Langley was very well connected. His fields included some of the most powerful men in government and business, including Andrew Carnegie and Alexander Graham Bell. He was also extremely well-funded. The

War Department, the precursor of the Department of Defense, had given him $50,000 in 1901 for the project (around $2,000,000 today).

The *New York Times* followed him everywhere. He gathered some of the most brilliant minds of the time to work on the project. Langley wanted to be the first to invent the flying machine. He wanted the kind of fame men like Thomas Edison had achieved after their invention. But with all the support and resources Langley had, the question is, why did he not complete his project?

One, he gave up after he failed and said it was impossible. Secondly, he was completely outworked, out-thought, and out-maneuvered by two brothers who despite their failures and modest resources, were rich in the most important attribute of all: mental strength.

Embrace your failures, learn from them and let them motivate you to push forward to the end. This is critical if you want to walk tall.

Every Decision Matters

We're always just one decision away from a totally different life. Every decision counts! Every decision! Every action! Every choice counts! Every choice that is made in your present moment has an impact on your future. Don't ever forget this! Because it's one of the most powerful principles you can live by. Every time you decide to work on yourself, instead of taking the easy road, that is a stronger you in the future!

When you decide to develop your mind by learning something new, rather than watching the news, that is a stronger, better you in the future. When you decide to eat healthy, rather than give in to the temptation to feed your body with foods that only do harm… stronger you in the future. When you decide to be kind, rather than fight a useless battle to defend your position…stronger, better you in the future. When you decide to rise early and meditate, there is a stronger and better you ready for the future. When you decide to keep going despite setbacks — stronger, better you in the future! When you decide to write down every day what you are grateful for, rather than complain about what is not there — a stronger better you in the future.

Every decision and every action matters! Every action has a consequence in the future both ways: good and bad. So yes, this one time does matter! Yes, that one sleep-in does matter! Habits matter! You matter! From now on decide to make conscious decisions! Powerful decisions every day! Set the standard and continue to raise the bar in your life!

Your positive actions will compound on themselves and soon you won't recognize the person you see in the mirror. The changes can be that great. You can be that great!

Chapter Two

YOU CAN LIVE A WORRY-FREE LIFE

There is nothing we cannot do if we know how, and everything is difficult and impossible to the person who does not know how to do it. Driving a car or swimming seems impossible and is difficult for a young person or a learner until he or she is taught how to drive or swim.

Can you imagine living in a time before electricity? How on earth did people survive? What about the airplane? Where did someone get the courage to imagine that human beings could fly? If I was living in a less civilized age and someone told me that a day would come when people would fly to far-off countries and across oceans, what would I have said? Sincerely, "impossible!"

> "A man does not live a hundred
>
> Yet he worries for a thousand..."
>
> — *Fred Addo*

Well, what would you say if I told you that you can live a life without worrying? Please don't say "impossible!" Because history has proved that it can be done. Nothing is impossible when you know how.

There is no mental attitude more disastrous to our personal achievements, happiness, and usefulness, than worry. To conquer worry, we must give it a bad name. Unfortunately, worry is more dangerous than many people think. It is not just a little flaw in someone's character or a negligible behavioral challenge. Worry is bad, satanic and poisonous.

Are you living a life of peace? To live in peace is to live a life of rest. Hebrews 4:11 tells us to make every effort to enter the rest of God. What this means is that we must actively guard our peace. You see, life is full of peace stealers. Every day there are people and circumstances that can pull you out of rest. However, you can learn how to put up boundaries and not allow everything in. You can learn to identify the peace stealers in your life and learn how to take care of your emotional energy. Even during difficulties and trials, you can learn how God wants to fight your battles for you! All you need to do is rest in Him!

It's tempting to jump into worrying when things go wrong, bad things happen or when difficulties arise. Many people worry, but it has never solved the problems, yet they worry all the same. Wisdom teachers tell us that we cannot keep doing things in the same way and expect a different result.

"Worry does not empty tomorrow of its sorrow.

It empties today of its strength."

*— **Corrie Ten Boom***

Let me inform you that worry is a vote of no confidence in God. It is trying to handle by yourself the very life you claim to have given to Jesus.

Worry is an indirect way of telling God that He is incompetent and not dependable.

Until we see worry as a dangerous habit, we are likely to pet it and even talk about it, without any real commitment to fight it. This thing called worry is usually about something that has not happened, but we are afraid and so sure that it will happen. It is amazing how the unknown and unseen can leave us sad, afraid, and without sleep; we suffer pain and sorrow because we anticipate hopelessness and pain even before they show up.

"How much pain they have cost us,

The evils which have never happened."

—*Thomas Jefferson*

I would like you to know that worry is a thief that wants to sneak into your life; shut the door of your mind and don't let worry in. Worry is a product of fear, and it comes like a seed and ends up a big forest. The more you worry, the more you become addicted to the habit. I know people who even worry because they have not worried for a while. And there are some who may become unhappy with you because you refuse to worry.

You may have heard this kind of statement before: "Can you believe she is 40 years old and still not married? And the girl is not even worrying about it?"

This ought not to be! Many people see worry as a necessary response to life's pressure and tough times. We tolerate and even feel sorry for people who worry, but that does not make a positive mindset.

Worry is not a problem solver; in fact, it creates bigger problems. It affects your health, your peace of mind, your joy, and indeed your whole life. As contagious and infectious as worry is, as widespread as worry has become, make no mistake; it is a dangerous habit and reduces your life span and mental well-being.

Worry takes away from your enthusiasm. It steals your drive and determination. It takes away your passion for action. It steals your peace, your health, and above all your ability to make good of what you have and appreciate what you are blessed with. The Bible says in Proverbs 17:22, (NIV), *"A cheerful heart does good like medicine, but a broken spirit makes one sick."* Tough times will always come. It is unavoidable; but you can choose to live worry-free even in tough times.

Some of the people who complain about being in an unhappy marriage do not realize that part of the reason their marriage is unhappy is because they are unhappy people. Worry makes people very negative, and people who worry a lot usually have unhealthy relationships. Worried people are not only preoccupied with themselves and their problems, they are touchy, overly sensitive.

"There is nothing that wastes the body like worry,

And one who has any faith in God should be ashamed

To worry about anything whatsoever."

— *Mahatma Gandhi*

Worry Attracts Trouble

Worry is a thief of God's blessings, because worry is a by-product of unbelief, and God has never gotten along with people who have no faith. Remember also that the Bible tells us that anything that does not proceed from faith is sin. The question is why would God be anxious to bless someone who is living in sin? According to Romans 14:23 (New King James Version, NKJV), *"But he who doubts is condemned if he eats, because he does not eat from faith; for whatsoever is not from faith is sin."*

Have you realized that most of the things people worry about have not even happened yet? Worrying is expecting the worst to happen, and many times, the worst does not happen. It is anxious thought (worry) that makes our days evil, not the other way around. People don't worry because evil things happen, rather evil things happen because people worry. By fearing the worst and expecting things to go wrong, we attract negative things into our lives.

> *"Worrying is arrogant,*
>
> *because God knows what He's doing."*
>
> — *Barbara Cameron*

It's time to cheer up and investigate the future with confidence; you can still break forth. Don't give up. As you continue with this book, I will share with you practical experience I have gained from going through tough tunnels in life as a young man born into a poor home; my father died just as I got into college, leaving my poor mum, a mother of four boys and a girl, with no job or professional training. I did all manner of hard jobs to be able to feed myself, pay my tuition and that of my four younger siblings who all depended on me for strength and motivation.

So, I'm not just sharing with you head knowledge or random motivation; rather I intend to communicate practical knowledge and tools that helped me stand strong during my tough times in life.

> *"People don't worry because evil things happen,*
>
> *rather evil things happen because people worry."*
>
> — *Fred Addo*

Most people I know do not worry because they love to do it; I don't know too many people who consider worry a good thing. And it does not take much spirituality for Christians to realize that worry is not approved by God. So why do people worry? They do it because they think that they must. Most people wish they could get rid of the habit because worry is not fun, and nobody enjoys it. Worry is a problem to those who worry, as well as a problem to those around the people who worry. But sometimes people do something for so long that they think it is normal.

There are many people who see worry as a natural reaction to presumed danger. If you try to stop people from worrying, they will probably tell you that if you were in the same situation, you would also be worried. The truth is that worry is not a reflex action but rather a choice.

> *"As a rule, men worry more about what they can't see*
>
> *Than about what they can."*
>
> *— Julius Caesar*

There is nothing natural or indeed universal about worry. If it was a natural reflex to pressure, then everybody would act the same way under the same circumstances. But we know that people have different responses to the same issue.

If worry is a choice, then we can choose to stop it. Jesus told us categorically in Matthew 6 that we should not worry. He even said we should not borrow this culture from the heathen and gentiles. In the book of Philippians, the word of God tells us not to worry about anything. *"Don't worry about anything; instead pray about everything; tell God your needs, and don't forget to thank him for his answers.* (Philippians 4:6, NIV).

Think about it, why would God tell us not to worry if we couldn't stop it? Why would Jesus rebuke us and say to those who worried, *"you of little faith"* (Matthew 6:30) if we had no choice but to worry? Why would Jesus embarrass us by comparing us with the lilies of the field and with birds that seem to do better than us who worry? Why would He do that if worry is something we can't stop?

"Worry is carrying tomorrow's load with today's strength—carrying two days at once.

It is moving into tomorrow ahead of time."

— **Corrie Ten Boom**

Warriors and Worriers

Those who worry too much are not doing so because they have a certain genetic frailty; they are doing so because they have a spiritual and emotional vulnerability. The second part of Daniel 11:32 (New King James Version, NKJV) says that *"the people who know their God shall be strong, and carry out great exploits."*

Knowledge helps make us strong, and the knowledge of God produces such inner strength and emotional stability that it makes worry ineffective. It is also true that the contagious and infectious nature of worry can make it as strong as a hereditary trait. By this I mean that the bad habit called worry can be passed through generations.

Don't get me wrong, this is not a spiritual warfare issue and I'm not talking about curses here. This is simply a case of *"train up a child in the way he should go, and when he is old, he will not depart from it."* (Proverbs 22:6 NKJV). Sometimes you can have whole families who are experts at worrying; a family of worriers. Warriors are people who fight back when things go wrong and never give up until they overcome. True warriors have that never-say-never spirit, they never give up or give in.

On the other hand, worriers prefer to give up and back out, and they take the advantage of every little problem to buy sympathy and cheap attention from everybody.

"I remember the story of the old man who said on his deathbed that he had had a lot of trouble in his life, most of which never happened."

— *Winston Churchill*

Remember that there is nobody on this planet without troubles and challenges; the only difference is that some worry about them and others solve them.

God wants His children to have a fighting spirit. When evil shows up, we should seek to overcome it and not let it overcome us. When we worry, we are declaring evil victorious over us. Note that it's not our problems that make us worry, it's our decisions and how we react to our problems. We can choose to worry about our problems or choose to have hope and confidence in the God we serve.

Don't let any situation pull you down. Be a fighter not a loser. Learn to respond, don't just react. People who worry (worriers) cannot say how their day is going to turn out. They are slaves to what might happen. They may leave home in the morning with a good attitude, but by evening a negative thought has dropped into their minds or they allow someone to plant fear, and they become miserable and that misery tends to sap strength from them.

"Worry is like a rocking chair;

it keeps you moving but doesn't get you anywhere."

— *Erma Bombeck*

Growing up as a young man, I went through storms that could have killed my zeal and determination to pursue destiny, but I decided not to let my storms pull me down. I chose to fight and fight till I win. Not with guns, swords, or any form of weapon but with my mind, willpower and faith in myself and my God.

I came across a very remarkable podcast on social media some years ago and it helped me a lot and changed my perspective towards life's ups and downs. This I will share with you in the next chapter.

> *"Life's challenges are not supposed to paralyze you;*
>
> *They're supposed to help you discover who you are."*
>
> *— **Bernice Reagan***

Chapter Three

A LITTLE SMILE CAN CHANGE A LOT

"We don't laugh on the same joke again,

why do we cry on the same problem again?"

— *Gaur Gopal Das*

Do you know the most pleasing five letter word? It is called "smile." It increases your face value and gives you boldness and confidence. We don't laugh on the same joke again, so why do we cry or worry on the same problem again? There will always be a reason to cry, but you can choose to respond to life's challenges in a different way. It all depends on you whether you want to cry tears in fear and defeat or smile and laugh in victory and internal peace.

I remember following a slide a friend sent me. When followed in life, I guarantee you, life will be different. The stimulation goes this way. Do you have a problem in life? Yes? Can you do something about it? Yes, then why worry? Do you have a problem in life? Yes? Can you do something about it? No? Then why worry?

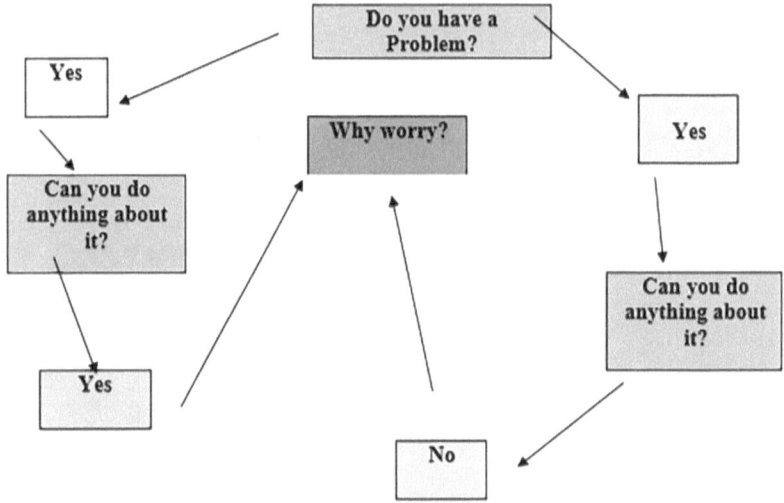

Why are we constantly bogging our minds with anxiety that won't allow us have peace of mind? We don't have control over what is happening around us or with us; but we have control over one thing, which is, "smile". A little smile can turn everything around. I have learned that when times are rough, the worst thing you can do is dwell on what is going on. It's hard, but you can't allow the storms you face to control your life. Focusing on them will suck all the life out of you, mentally and physically.

I have seen people who just stop living because they are too focused on the issues that they are dealing with. They lock themselves inside, never want to get out of bed, and try to shut out everyone and everything. This type of behavior only adds to the problems that you are going through.

When the storms in life come, focus on the many other blessings in your life. Also, think about the many times you thought everything was falling apart, but somehow you made it through. It's never the end unless you give up and stop fighting. No matter what you go through your joy is worth the fight. Life is too short to let anything or anyone steal your joy.

A smile conveys feelings of happiness, hope and positivity to anyone who sees it. When you smile, you are sending a message to those around you: you are accepted, you are welcome, and all is well. In a world full of reasons to brood and be upset, there is only one thing that can bring in some hope. A wide, bright, smile.

Mother Teresa once said, "Every time you smile at someone, it is an action of love, a gift to that person, a beautiful thing!" It is so true. Even when you are having a bad day or things aren't going the way you want them to, a simple smile, even from someone whom you may not know, can make your day better. Such a simple thing and yet it has an effect that can turn your entire day around.

Learning to Laugh in the Face of Adversity

I wonder when you last had a deep belly laugh where your whole body shook helplessly. I think those rivers of living water that the Holy Spirit floods and fills our being with as believers in Christ must at least bubble up sometimes as holy joy, if not laughter. It's so sweet how babies can chuckle/laugh up to 300 times a day, whereas weary adults barely make it to 20 times a week. Have you forgotten how to let loose? Lost touch with inner joy?

I see Jesus as a joy-bringer, someone who must have laughed a lot while here on earth. I picture Him chuckling with His disciples, smiling and laughing as He took infants into His arms and cradled children on His lap. Not like fake jovial Christmas, but as a reflection of the freedom and zest which living a Spirit-filled life can bring to you.

"Knowing God as prodigal-loving, exuberantly generous,

All-giving father is enough reason to rejoice."

— Joy Lenton

Religion can seem dry, dutiful and dreary. Theology can be dull and dusty too, but God gives us much to be thankful for in our everyday lives. Jack London, one of the most well-known authors in American history, was famous for his adventure novels, like *White Fang* and *The*

Call of the World. He is less known, however, for his commentary on boxing matches, though there may be much we can learn from his words. After sitting in the audience of a 1910 boxing match between Jack Johnson and then reigning world champion Jim Jeffries, London wrote "no one understands him, this man who smiles. Well, the story of the fight is the story of a smile. If ever a man won by nothing more fatiguing than smile, Johnson won today."

Johnson went on to defeat Jeffries, all while wearing a smile on his face. London's words may have just been a simple observation of a fight, but what he wrote can be a remarkable metaphor for life overall.

Just as Ryan Holiday, American author, media strategist and entrepreneur writes, "the world is going to try to knock us down. We will face unfairness, animus, even evil. How will we respond? With anger? With rage? By letting it get to us?"

Well, why not try responding with a smile? With excitement? For you, it can uplift your mood, and push you to keep going. For your opponents, or those in your life who are causing you trouble, your smile or laughter may look deranged, and it will confuse them. At this point of confusion, you may be able to claim a victory.

> *"How do you beat someone you can't even get to?*
>
> *That gets happier the more you throw at them?"*
>
> — *Ryan Holiday*

Smiling is number 2 on the list of the 43 habits of happy people. If you can turn smiling into a habit, then you can turn happiness into a habit.

You're Most Attractive!

Do you want to be more attractive? Simply smile! Research has proven that we find others more attractive when they are wearing a smile. This one is a no-brainer, but for the sake of helping it take root in your mind, think about someone who you know. First, think of when they are down, sad, angry, frustrated, whatever it may be. How attractive are they?

Now picture them simply with a smile on their face. What does this do to their attractiveness? If you took the time to do this exercise, I'm sure you would have easily found the smiling version much more attractive, and maybe this even made you feel a happy tingle inside yourself!

A Smile is Contagious

Have you ever been in a sour mood and had someone come along with a huge smile, some laughter, or a good mood? Perhaps a baby that just looked up at you and smiled? How did this make you feel? When the person you are talking to or the people that surround you are smiling, you won't be able to help but smile! A smile has special powers. You can calm fear, insecurity, hurt, and anxiety not only in yourself, but in others experiencing those feelings. The next time someone is feeling sad, scared, nervous, whatever it may be, smile with them and see how this makes them feel!

Even 2Pac, the deceased rap legend, realized the benefits of smiling. In "Power of a Smile" he raps:

"The power of a gun can kill.

The power of the mind can learn.

The power of anger can rise inside until it tears you apart.

But the power of a smile, especially yours, 2 Pac

Can heal a frozen heart."

A smile is a contagious thing. Give to the world and the world will give back to you. Smile at the world and the world will smile back at you.

You will brighten the days of those around and make a difference in their lives, simply by smiling! You also use fewer muscles to smile than you do for frowning. Hopefully you're smiling now as you read this, but if not, smile now! Now that you have tried smiling, try and frown. Which one do you think is easier? I would say smiling is the easier of the two, and also stretches your muscles and skin less throughout life, helping you age gracefully.

Research has shown that smiling releases serotonin, a neurotransmitter that produces feelings of happiness and wellbeing. It's like a circle of happiness.

Build Better, Faster, Relationships

Smiling is such a key ingredient for establishing healthy and genuine friendship. When someone is smiling at you it indicates that they like you. When someone likes you what do you think of them? Yep, normally you're thinking, "Wow, I like this person!" Smiling offers encouragement to the person that you are talking to. Think about it. If someone is smiling at you while you are talking to them, you feel as though they are totally into what you are saying, encouraging you to keep going!

Life poses many challenges, but the way of the wise is to just accept every challenge and move through with a smile.

We lose money; we can lose a home, relationship, job, or even a leg and still have hope. But if we lose our ability to smile, we have indeed lost a great power in us. Terrible things will always come our way on earth. Yours could be a sudden betrayal or a broken relationship, and you can choose to smile at it. I know it can be tough to smile when challenges and pain arise, but if you can master this art, I assure you, nothing can defeat you.

I read a story of some Biafra soldiers who were ambushed in the thick rain forest during the Nigerian civil war. This group of zealous but poorly trained Igbo foot soldiers had run out of bullets for their locally made wooden guns. They were surrounded by the heavily armed Nigerian soldiers, who were instructed to kill on sight, but suddenly these Biafra soldiers burst into laughter, and their laughter became louder as they marched towards the armed Nigerian soldiers.

The Nigerian soldiers, thinking that the Biafra soldiers had been possessed by a juju spirit (African Voodoo), ran for their lives, and some even threw away their weapons. That is the power of laughter. It drives away pains and brings boldness and mental stability.

"Happiness is not the absence of problems;

It's the ability to deal with them."

— Steve Maraboli

Friend, I want you to know that tough times and challenges are part and parcel of life. But that does not mean that we should completely focus on the problems and forget to smile. In other words, if we remain sad or grumpy due to the problems, we are letting the problems control how we feel.

In fact, deciding to be happy despite having problems means that you are choosing to keep yourself in positive state of mind while facing the problems in your life. Based on my experience I can tell you that if you adopt this attitude, you will be able to deal with your problems objectively and effectively, and solve most of them.

> *"If life gives you 100 reasons to cry,*
>
> *Show life that you have 1000 reasons to smile."*
>
> — **Bishop Harry Jackson**

Today, you can choose to smile at life's ups and downs. Remember that we don't smile to hide our pain; rather we smile to heal it. I hope you smile today.

Chapter Four

PEACE AMID STORMS

Have you ever been in a hurricane? In the centre of the hurricane, there's something called the "eye of the storm" where it's very calm and peaceful. All around there is chaos, winds blowing 100 plus miles an hour, debris flying left and right, danger everywhere, but if you're in the eye of the storm, it's as calm and peaceful as can be. Peace is not the absence of trouble, but the absolute calmness and tranquility amidst the storm.

Have you ever thought your heart and mind couldn't be at peace because your circumstances were far from peaceful? I have good news for you my friend. Peace is available during less than peaceful circumstances. Considering life will always present circumstances and problems that threaten to steal our peace and fill our hearts and minds with negative thoughts, this is great news for God's children.

Scripture tells us in John 16:33 that in this life we will have troubles, but Jesus Himself told us not to fear for He Himself has overcome the world for us. Peace is a gift, a gift from God to those who receive Him by receiving His Son Jesus Christ into their hearts and lives. Once you have Jesus, you will have peace in your heart, and then you can release that inner peace to affect your mental state during tough times.

The truth is this: no Jesus, no peace! Know Jesus, know peace. When we find peace with God, it is easier to find peace in life.

"When we are unable to find tranquility

Within ourselves, it is useless to seek it elsewhere."

— ***Francois de La Rochefoucauld***

Peace flows from inside outward, not the other way around. If you don't have peace inside, then you don't have it. Peace is arguably the most sought-after concept on the planet. People seek lovely, "peaceful" scenery not knowing that peace cannot be found in a place. There may be beauty and silence all around, yet turbulence in the mind. Peace is not the absence of crisis; it is the ability to be surprisingly calm despite the crisis.

The ability to be calm during uncertainty, lack, financial crisis, death of a loved one, loss of a home or job, or a sudden broken relationship, comes to those who have anchored their hope in Christ. Worry like we saw earlier, finds its strength in insecurity and lack of assurance. But those who have Christ find confidence in the fact that He will never forsake them and that He can make a way where there seems to be no way. The strongest people are not those who show strength in front of us but those who win battles others know nothing about and yet remain calm.

This world is a place of tribulation and confusion, a world of fear, worry, and uncertainty. But the kingdom of God is different, and you can start experiencing Heaven here on earth. It is the kingdom of joy and peace that every child of God enjoys in the Holy Spirit. The Bible says in Romans 14:17 (NKJV) *"for the kingdom of God is not eating and drinking, but righteousness and peace and joy in the Holy Spirit."*

All too often, when we're going through rough times, well-meaning people try to reassure us by quoting the all-too-popular "God will not give us more than we can handle," cliché, and I bet you've heard or been told that before. But the truth is, nowhere in scripture do we find that saying. In fact, Bible says just the opposite.

The disciples alone experienced so many troubles and serious hardships, physically, mentally, spiritually, and emotionally that it makes one wonder how they carried such heavy loads and managed to stay bold, faithful and strengthened in the face of such never ending adversity. But we all know, they weren't doing life alone. They had Jesus. And so do us.

The confusion about the phrase, "God will never give us more than we can handle" most likely originates from 1 Corinthians 10:13 (NLT) which says, *"The temptations in your life are no different from what others experience. And God is faithful. He will not allow the temptation to be more than you can stand. When you are tempted, he will show you a way out so that you can endure."* Notice this verse mentions temptations, not burdens.

The truth is that there may still come a time when you feel God has given you more than you can handle. And honestly, physically those problems just might be more than we can handle. More than our heart can bear, and our faith can carry. More than we can process mentally without being afraid. Negativity, pessimism, frustration and maybe even hopelessness may begin to root deeply into the recesses of our minds. Somehow the negative happenings of life just seem like too much. But nothing is ever too much for God, or too much for us if we learn to trust in Him.

"Sometimes it takes only adversities to

Put us right where God wants us to be,

In the position of seeking his presence."

— Billy Graham

I don't know about you, but I've certainly experienced painful circumstances and adversities that I thought were more than I could handle. Times when I wasn't happy with God about all I was going through. Times when I found myself wondering if God had indeed given me more than I could bear. Wondering if my past would sting my heart forever.

Wondering if the weight of the hurt that others inflicted upon me could ever be lifted. Wondering if I could ever forgive those who had betrayed and abandoned me and my siblings when my dad died and left us with nothing. Wondering why my uncles and aunties so hated me and my siblings that they chose to abandon us.

Wondering if the situations I was facing would ever end or be resolved and doubting they could ever be used for God's good, much less His good in my life. Sometimes even wondering if I might get crushed under the weight of my negative thoughts and emotions as I contemplated just wanting to give up hope entirely.

I love how The Message Bible (MSG) reminds us of God's holy promise and instructs us about what to do when we're at the end of our rope and negativity is consuming our every thought. We find this instruction in Psalm 55:22, *"Pile your troubles on God's shoulders—he'll carry your load, he'll help you out. He'll never let good people topple in ruin."*

In the scripture above, we see David complaining to God about the heartache and fear resulting from the betrayal of friends, and the hatred of his enemies who were after him. His burdens seemed overwhelming, and in utter despair he poured his concerns out to God. Yet what is so amazing is that in the same breath, we also see him choosing to pile those troubles onto God's shoulders, committing to trust and believe He would bring victory and help. You see, David changed his attitude, and it immediately changed his life.

> *"When we control our thoughts instead of Letting them control us, positive changes pour in."*
>
> *— Tracie Miles*

Our enemies are probably different from David's. Instead of people, they may be sin, regrets of the past, feelings of unworthiness, or difficult and painful circumstances; our enemies may be stressful situations at work, hurtful co-workers, racism, broken marriage, prodigal children, death of a loved one, or financial bankruptcy. But like David, we too can find comfort and spiritual healing if we believe God is with us; patiently waiting for us to depend on Him and lay down the emotional weights we are shouldering.

When we find healing in our minds, it opens the door for us to begin thinking positively even if life doesn't appear to warrant it.

> *"Nothing is more beautiful than a smile that has struggled through tears."*
>
> *— Demi Lovato*

Life can be hard. The past can grip our hearts. Memories can be painful. Burdens can feel heavy. Regrets can feel suffocating. Emotions can seem overwhelming. Situations can seem hopeless and more than you can bear. But even during the fiercest raging storms, it is possible to think positive thoughts, live a positive life, and have an unsinkable faith just like David's. It's all a matter of choosing to do so, despite the "enemies" around us.

We can control our thoughts, which helps us fight the battles we face each day. The greatest fight is done in our minds and if we can win the battle of our minds, then we surely will experience total peace outside. If you choose to think negative, you will feel negative, and live negative, and a negative mind will never lead to a positive life of victory.

"The tiny seed knew that to grow,

It needed to be dropped in dirt,

Covered in darkness and struggle to reach the light."

— Sandra Kring

Learn From the Master Himself: Jesus Christ

Life is composed of ups and downs. Learning to get through the downs is key to being successful. Without obstacles, difficulties, struggles, and challenges, life wouldn't make much sense. You become stronger, more compassionate, and more grateful when you strongly believe in your capacity to persevere. The most successful people know what it's like to persevere and savor victory, personally and professionally, and so can you.

Out of nowhere the storms of life strike. Without warning and without mercy, crippled by a car accident, disabled by an illness, abandoned by a loved one, home destroyed by flood, fire or tornado, job termination, loss of a loved one, financial bankruptcy, broken relationships, and lots more.

The storms of life strike without compassion. Jesus and His disciples were caught unexpectedly one night in the storm as recorded in Mark 4:35-41(NIV), it reads:

That day when evening came, he said to his disciples, "Let us go over to the other side." Leaving the crowd behind, they took him along, just as he was, in the boat. There were also other boats with him. A furious squall came up, and the waves broke over the boat, so that it was nearly swamped. Jesus was in the stern, sleeping on a cushion. The disciples woke him and said to him, "Teacher, don't you care if we drown?"

He got up, rebuked the wind and said to the waves, "Quiet! Be still!" Then the wind died down and it was completely calm. He said to his disciples, "Why are you so afraid? Do you still have no faith?" They were terrified and asked each other, "Who is this? Even the wind and the waves obey him!"

He hasn't changed! Let's notice some truths that we can apply to our lives. The storms of life are perilous and unexpected. Jesus and His disciples had planned to cross the lake. Many times, the disciples had tossed their nets there, as was their custom. Now, they routinely set out across the lake. Characteristically of the Sea of Galilee, a furious storm suddenly engulfed the tiny boat.

> "Keep the faith, hold on. Things will get better.
>
> It might be stormy now, but it can't rain forever."
>
> — *Great Igwe*

Even today these dreaded storms are treacherous, sinking unsuspecting boaters. You don't have to be in the middle of the Sea of Galilee to be taken by surprise by the storms of life. Retirees struggle to keep their heads above the waters of inflation, millions drowning in a sea of alcoholism and prescription drug addiction, others swamped by endless hours of loneliness, waves of insecurity, and swelling tides of uselessness. How are you coping with these storms? How do you calm the roaring sea of life?

Jesus can calm the storms raging in our beleaguered hearts. Storms that threaten to swallow society, families and nations. But right now, are we able to smile amidst the storms?

The truth is that some of the storms we face in life as individuals, families, communities or nations, we can't handle alone. Just like the disciples asked Jesus; "Teacher, don't you care if we drown?" Look at those fishermen, hardy men of the sea. They loved the water. The water was their livelihood, their home, their life and best friend. They were at home on the water.

People need to make a determined effort to be able to live in peace because there will always be challenges that will undermine their peace of mind. If you're going to live in peace, it's not going to happen by accident. Every day, we have opportunities to get upset, be offended, and live worried. Life happens. People get on your nerves. Unexpected bills come.

God never promised that He would keep us from difficulties. He never said that we wouldn't have storms. But He did say that He would give us peace during the storms. He calls it a "peace that passes understanding". What God means by this, is that people will always have peace even though everything in their lives appears to be going crazy. Your mind needs a break. It wasn't meant to go all the time. The scripture says, "Cast your cares on the Lord." You have to learn to turn that mess over to God. You weren't designed to carry a heavy load. It will frustrate you.

The key to this is knowing that God works while people rest and God rests when people work. Joel Osteen says people need to take a step back sometimes and let God handle things. "That's when God goes to work, and you can enjoy life living in peace!" he says.

Call Out to God for Help Before You Sink

God allows problems to come into our lives. It's not that He gives us problems, but that He lets them pass through the funnel. Why? Because problems are supposed to make you believe. Without trials and persecutions, there would be no need for us to exercise faith, but in gaining problems, we gain reasons to believe that despite these problems, we know that there is a God who is above the situation and who has a good, pleasing and perfect will for us.

Do you want to sink before you call out to God for help? Are we so stubborn? So blind? Pride prevents us from acknowledging reality.

Suppose we decide to relinquish the oars, could things get worse? The disciples didn't know Jesus could calm the storm. They didn't expect Him to still the sea. But they had nowhere else to turn. All else had failed. Before going under they turned to Jesus. All they did was turn to Jesus and give Him the opportunity. What about you? Ready to let Jesus have a turn at the wheel?

"Storms make trees take deeper roots."

— Dolly Parton

The Voyage of the Mayflower

Years ago, a made-for-TV movie told the story of the pilgrims crossing the Atlantic Ocean to build a new home in America. Throughout the journey the captain and crew ridiculed and taunted the "foolish landlubbers". What did farmers know anyhow?

During the voyage the ship was caught in a storm. "You farmers hide below. We'll brave the storm on deck." The Mayflower bounced around like a cork, its frail old timbers weakening from the onslaught of wind and waves. Suddenly a sickening crack. The pilgrims who were down below called out to the captain, as the main beam cracked and began to give way. Somberly, the captain said, "The old gal's back is broken. In a few minutes she'll break into pieces."

One of the pilgrims excitedly shouted, "What if we put our iron jack under the beam?"

"What do you people think you can do?" shot back the captain. "Nothing can push this beam back into place or much less support such stress."

"We've nothing to lose," said the pilgrim. "Let's try it!"

"Go ahead landlubber," said the captain. "It'll keep you busy till the water fills your lungs."

Feverishly they unpacked the jack and wedged it into place. It worked! Captain and crew couldn't believe it. With newfound appreciation the experts had to rethink their opinion. You know the rest of the story. The pilgrims landed at Plymouth Rock.

> *"Before the storms of life sink you,*
>
> *Give Jesus a chance."*
>
> — ***Great Igwe***

Jesus will see us safely through the storms of life because He is peace personified. While the storm howled about Him, He rested comfortably. He wasn't frantically chewing His fingernails, searching for another chain cigarette, or reaching for another drink to deaden reality. Jesus was peacefully asleep, unaffected by the rocking of the boat, yelling of the crew, spraying of cold water and howling of the wind; none of that woke Him. The disciples were miffed. How could Jesus be so indifferent? Doesn't He care if we drown? *We're about to die, everything coming apart at the seams. Nothing is going right. How can He sleep?* The disciples go to wake Jesus. Instantly, upon their touch, Jesus responded to their beckoning.

How many times have you seen a mother sound at sleep with the TV blaring, kids stampeding, trucks and trail bikes passing outside the window and somehow, she manages to sleep through the noise undisturbed? Yet at the other end of the house her baby sighs and instantly, mom rushes to her child.

Jesus reacted immediately to the disciples' cries. Immediately, He stopped the storm and calmed the sea. It was harder for Jesus to calm their hearts. The storm worried them. The calm terrified them. It's much harder for God to calm the souls of people than the waves of the sea. It's easier for God to move mountains and part the oceans than quiet the troubled heart. Nature must obey God's commands, but God needs permission to calm the heart of men.

What about you? Will you allow God to calm your storm-tossed life? Ulcer? Diabetes, cancer, recurring headaches? Financial concerns? Jesus asks, "Why are you so afraid? Have you still no faith? Don't you understand that as long as I'm with you there is no need to fear?"

The lyricist Mary Ann Baker wrote in the hymn, "Master the Tempest is Raging",

---

"No waters can swallow the ship where lays,

the master of ocean, and earth, and skies."

T.L Osborn

Whatever your difficulty, you have two options: you can worry and assume that Jesus no longer cares. Or you can resist fear and put your trust in Him. When you feel like panicking, confess your need for God, and then trust Him to care for you.

See Jesus lying in the boat tired, exhausted, energy drained from healing and teaching all day. Yet, weak as He was, see Him stand. See Him command nature to be still. The resurrected Christ told us, "All power and authority in heaven and earth are given to me." In other words, Jesus says to us, "I'm in charge. I'm in control. Why do you fear? Why does anxiety gnaw away at you?" In proportion as we really know Jesus, in that proportion we will be at peace. Do you know Jesus well enough to smile amidst the storms?

> *"As we pour out our bitterness,*
>
> *God pours in his peace."*
>
> — **F.B. Meyer**

Christ may allow storms, but He accompanies us. No need for the disciples to wake Jesus. In fact, Jesus didn't want the disciples to wake Him. He wanted them to learn by watching Him in the storm. Keep your eyes on Christ amidst the storms. Look hard upon Him. He can calm the storm, yes, but what can we learn as He accompanies us through times of trouble? When we truly understand who Jesus Christ is, we will realize that He controls both the storms of nature and the storms of the troubled heart.

How do you react to danger and stress? The same power that calmed the storms can also help you deal with the problems you face. Jesus is willing to help if you only ask Him. Never discount His power, even in terrible trials. What is the need of faith if you never test it? Who needs faith when the sailing is smooth, the skies are clear?

Jesus asks, "Why are you so afraid? Have you still no faith?"

Are you able to smile amidst the storms? Jesus will see you safely through the storms of life.

> *"I have held many things in my hands,*
>
> *And have lost them all; but whatever I*
>
> *Have placed in God's hands, that I still possess."*
>
> — **Martin Luther**

The world today is one big storm. Individuals, families, and nations are threatening to sink. However, we are safer in the middle of the storm with Jesus than anywhere else without Him. You can experience peace. With Jesus as the captain of our ship, we may navigate life smiling amidst the storm. Facing a storm in your life? So, you've already tried the booze, pills and everything else. Maybe now is the time to ask Jesus to calm the storms in your life.

Sometimes life is like a disappointing mess of confusing pieces. The longer we sit staring at the fragments, the more hopeless it all seems. But when we remember His word in Psalm 46:10, *"Be still and know that I am God"*, we are comforted knowing that He will make something beautiful out of the mess of our lives. The Hebrew phrase for "be still" literally means, "To put your hands down to the side; to relax." Which leads us to this reading of the phrase: "put your arms down and relax, knowing that I am God."

I don't know about you, but I sometimes find it hard to just "relax" during confusing and disheartening seasons of life. When things go haywire, when dreams are demolished, when family is fragmented, when people have pulverized us, it's hard to relax! Our instinct is to try to keep our hands on all the pieces at once. We want to manipulate and control them and force the outcome that we desire. But God says that we should do exactly the opposite. Stop trying to force the issue and let go. If we don't give up striving with the problems, our meddling usually just makes things worse.

"If God be our God, He will give us peace in trouble. When there is a storm without, He will make peace within. The world can create trouble in peace, but God can create peace in trouble."

*— **Thomas Watson**ns*

Thankfully, Psalm 46:10 calls on us to let go. But it's not letting go without knowing to whom we're letting it go. Notice that the verse says,

"Be still, and know." Normally, when life is a confusing puzzle, what we know is overshadowed by what we feel. Our emotions threaten to drown us like a scary tsunami. It's easy to get submerged in a wave of anxiety or a surge of self-pity. But notice that God says the only way we are going to be able to let go and relax is to remember who God is—and to know that He loves us, that He is not confused, that He is in the details, and that, as we obey and trust Him, He is working to make sense of it all.

When we allow ourselves to be taken in by the wonder of God's work in the mess of our lives, we will be free to stop fretting over the pieces knowing that in the end God is putting the pieces together so that the beauty will be perfect.

Chapter Five

UNSINKABLE FAITH

Faith: full assurance in the heart.

Life rarely ever goes exactly as planned. Often life will take you in a completely different direction from the path you intended to travel. No matter what happens, have faith! Faith that in the end, not right now, but, in the end, it will work out!

Faith is believing it will happen when there are no signs it will happen. Faith is believing in your dream when no one else does. Faith is sitting in the middle of the storm of your life and still being able to close your eyes and picture the sunny skies, still being able to feel the better days coming, despite the storm all around you. That's faith! Sometimes you may need to risk it all for a dream only you can see. Have faith in your dream, no matter what you must sacrifice to get there. No matter how long it is going to take: "I have faith this will work out in the end".

> *"If born of God, I have power to overcome*
>
> *All that is not of God."*
>
> *— G.V. Wigram*

Faith is taking the first step, even when you can't see the whole path. Trusting the rest of path will reveal itself in time…if you keep moving forward! Faith is stepping out there and having a crack when the conditions aren't perfect.

If you wait for the conditions to be perfect to go after the things you want, you might just be waiting forever! Einstein once said: "Only those who can see the invisible can achieve the impossible".

You must have faith that what you are picturing in your mind will come to life.

You must have faith that the struggle will pass! You must have faith your time will come! Because when you believe in yourself you are unstoppable!

Let your faith be bigger than your fear! Have faith, success will be near! Remember it may not happen immediately, but just know that in time it absolutely will happen. Long term, it's yours. Just keep believing and never lose faith! There is no greater asset than faith and belief in yourself.

It does not matter who you are right now, or who you have been. If you have faith and a relentless desire to succeed, you really can achieve anything in this world. Have faith you will be great and go get it.

For many people, remaining optimistic and feeling positive about themselves and their lives is a constant battle especially when circumstances are difficult, and life is hard. For others, negativity is something that only sneaks up from time to time, yet still wreaks havoc in their hearts. Regardless of the root causes, once pessimistic thoughts permeate our minds, our feelings and emotions begin to control us instead of us controlling them. Eventually it doesn't seem possible to stay positive, happy, and full of joy, and negative thought patterns shake our faith, causing us to sink emotionally, mentally, and spiritually over time. But it doesn't have to be that way.

> *"No matter what storm you face, you need to know that God loves you. He has not abandoned you."*
>
> — *Franklin Graham*

Despite what storms roll in, hearts anchored in God don't sink. When we change the way we think, we can change the way we feel and live, even if our circumstances remain the same. Intentionally embracing the opportunity to experience a transformed heart and a renewed mind opens the door for a changed life, because a positive mind will always lead to a more positive life.

Psalm 46:1 tells us, *"God is our refuge and strength, an ever-present help in trouble."* Regardless of your circumstances, God is with you and for you. Our God is not far off. This doesn't necessarily mean our troubles will disappear, but it does mean that God will walk with us through our trials. Like a good friend, God promises to stick with us and provide encouragement, hope, and a reminder of our potential through and beyond our current situation.

To trust God, we must first understand the nature of God and how He often works in our lives. God is sovereign over all, and His love and wisdom exceed anything we're fully capable of grasping. Consider Romans 8:35-39 (NIV). It says;

Who shall separate us from the love of Christ? Shall trouble or hardship or persecution or famine or nakedness or danger or sword? As it is written:

"For your sake we face death all day long;

We are considered as sheep to be slaughtered." No, in all these things we are more than conquerors through him who loved us. For I am convinced that neither death nor life, neither angels nor demons, neither the present nor the future, nor any powers, neither height nor depth, nor anything else in all creation, will be able to separate us from the love of God that is in Christ Jesus our Lord.

This passage makes it clear that God is all-powerful, nothing can hinder His love for us, and His desire is that we live victoriously in our lives. It's important to remember, however, that God's ways are higher than our ways. This often means that His timetable is different from our timetable. Even our answered prayers may look different from how we expect or hope they will look. Regardless of when or how God sees us through our hardships, we must trust that He is the one that ultimately knows what's best for us. Don't allow fear to drive you away from God; cling to Him in your trial!

"We must embrace pain and burn it as fuel for our journey."

— Kenji Miyazawa

Are you going through a hard time? Maybe you recently lost your job, or you're dealing with a death in your family. Or maybe you're just not sure anything good in life can happen to you. Whatever you're dealing with, I want you to know that you're not alone and something good can come from the tough spot you're in right now. God promised.

Chad Walsh wrote an intriguing book entitled *Early Christians of the Twenty-First Century*. He provoked my thinking with words like these:

"Millions of Christians live in a sentimental haze of vague piety, with soft organ music trembling in the lovely light from stained-glass windows. Their religion is a pleasant thing of emotional quiver, divorced from the intellect, divorced from the will, and demanding little except lip service to a few harmless platitudes.

I suspect that Satan has called off his attempt to convert people to agnosticism. After all, if a person travels far enough away from Christianity, he or she is always in danger of seeing it in perspective and deciding that it is true. It is much safer, from Satan's point of view, to vaccinate a person with a mild case of Christianity to protect him from the real disease."

Do you ever ask yourself, "Why is it that so many Christians have a mild case of Christianity?" I think the answer is this: an inadequate and imprecise view of faith. We tend to have a sloppy, spongy view of this critical subject. As it says in Hebrews 11:6, *"Without faith it is impossible to please God."* In other words, it's an absolute essential. But I believe the greatest error is to think that faith is unique to Christianity. It is not. God wove it into the system. And it is impossible to live without faith.

The last time you went to a doctor, he wrote out a little prescription. You couldn't read it. In fact, you wondered if anybody could read the thing! Then you took it to your pharmacist. Have you ever noticed when you give a pharmacist a prescription, he always disappears behind the screen? That shakes me up. I often wonder what in the world the guy is doing back there. I wonder if he slept through his course in pharmacy school. But he gives you the little bottle and says, "Take it three times a day" and by faith you do exactly what he tells you to do. That is the same faith I'm talking about here. Faith is woven into the system.

Learning Faith in the Marketplace

I'm going to show you a page out of our Lord's life. I've sometimes called this section "Christianity 101" because I think it deals with the kind of basic stuff that most of us are trying to get a handle on. Let me give you the context, because it's rich. Mark 4 verse 35 begins, "That day". That forces you to go back. What day? The day they heard the lectures on faith by the world's greatest teacher. But you don't learn faith by a lecture. You learn it in life. You don't learn it in church. You learn it in the marketplace.

> *"The way I see it, if you want the rainbow,*
>
> *You gotta put up with the rain."*
>
> — **Dolly Parton**

That day when evening came, Jesus said to His disciples, "Let's go to the other side". Leaving the crowd behind, they took Him along, just as He was, in the boat. There were also other boats with them. A furious squall came up, and the waves broke (literally, "kept breaking") over the boat, so that it was nearly swamped. Jesus was in the stern, sleeping on a cushion. And the disciples woke Him and said to Him, "Teacher, don't you care if we drown?"

Who said that? Not a seminary professor but a group of professional fishermen, who had spent their whole lives on that lake, who were experienced, who knew exactly how those storms came up.

The disciples had seen this many times. They had never seen one like this. As far as they were concerned, this was it. Things were desperate. So, Jesus got up, rebuked the wind and said to the waves, "Quiet! Be still!" (Literally, "be muzzled and remain so"). Then the wind died down, and it was completely calm.

> *"We must accept finite disappointment,*
>
> *But never lose infinite hope."*
>
> — *Martin Luther King, Jr.*

If you've ever been on the sea, if you are during a storm and that storm stops, the sea does not. It continues often for days. Here, you see, you have a two-fold miracle. Not only does the wind stop, the waves stop. Then in verse 40: "Jesus said to His disciples, 'why are you so afraid?'"

The Greeks were great communicators. So, when they wanted to emphasize a word, they would take it out of the normal word order, bring it up to the front of the sentence. This is like taking a red pencil and underlining it five times. That's what you have here: "How is it that you, of all people, are afraid?" Who? The guys who just heard the lecture. The guys who heard the Lord say, "He who has ears to hear, let him hear." They got a big 'F'. "Do you still have no faith?"

They were terrified and asked each other, "Who is this? Even the wind and the waves obey him!" Do you identify with them? Let's suppose one of those Texas tornadoes gets out of the alley, and it sweeps through where you are now, and suddenly the whole section of the building is off, and everyone right where you are is transfixed. And suddenly you hear someone get up and say, "Be still!" What would you do?

You'd turn to the guy or gal next to you and say, "Hey, man, the problem isn't up in the sky, it's up in his head!" But if suddenly it became still, you would begin to say to one another, "Who is this guy?"

Faith Depends Upon Its Object

I want to give you three lessons. The first lesson we learn about biblical faith is that biblical faith always depends upon its object. You can have little faith in thick ice, and you survive. You can have great faith in thin ice, and you drown. It's not the amount of faith. It's the object in which you place it.

That's why the Bible never says, "believe", it always says "believe on the Lord Jesus Christ." That's why the Bible never says, "Have faith", it always says, "Have faith in God." There's only one worthy object for faith, and His name is Jesus Christ. And the more you know of Him, the more you're going to cry out as the disciples did: "Who is this that even the wind and the waves obey him?"

> *"Only faith in a worthy object*
>
> *Can see us through hard times."*
>
> — **Howard Hendricks**

You're going to discover that God is very much interested in developing your faith, and that He's the perfect educator. He knows the ideal curriculum to make you like Jesus Christ. And He's going to allow some problems come into your life because He loves you. He loves you so much He not only accepts you as you are, but He loves you so much He will not allow you to remain the way you are. He has a wonderful plan to conform you to the image of Jesus Christ.

> *"God has a purpose behind every problem. He uses circumstances to develop our character. In fact, He depends more on circumstances to make us like Jesus than He depends on our reading the Bible."*
>
> — **Rick Warren**

Let's say I flew out from Dallas to San Jose. Let's suppose I said, "Maybe I could save myself some money." So, I look for some unsuspecting individual running around the Dallas airport and say to him, "Hey, man, would you fly me up to San Jose?"

'San Jose? Where's San Jose?"

"Well, I don't know all together, but it's out on the west coast a little south of San Francisco.

"Sure. I don't know where it is, but, yeah, I'll take you."

So we go over to what is supposed to be an airplane. We look at the thing, and the fuselage is held together with baling wire. Half of the tail assembly is gone. One wing is absent. The prop is bent. I say to him, "You have been up before, haven't you?"

He says, "No. As a matter of fact, I never have been. But I'm fascinated with flying. Hop in!"

If I get in that plane that is not faith. That's foolishness, because the object of my faith is worthless.

Who was it that said, "Let's go to the other side"? That's why when they see Him calm the storm, the disciples say, "Who is this?"

They not only heard what He said, they saw what He did. Jesus' miracles, His works, always authenticate His word. What He said and what He did were thoroughly compatible. (By the way, that's why you need to get to know Him.)

J. B. Phillips wrote an interesting book some years ago entitled, *Your God is Too Small*. That's our problem. I find that the more I get to know Him, the Person, the more my faith begins to grow. That's because it's then placed in a worthy object.

"God is as big as you think him to be.

If you see him small, he will manifest small,

But if you see him big, then he will divide the ocean

For you to pass through."

— *E.W Kenyon*

Faith is a Developmental Process

God is not simply interested in solving problems; He's interested in developing your faith. He knows exactly how to do that. I find that most Christians know only two things. They know the cross, and they know the coming of Jesus Christ. In the past, He died on the cross; in the future, He's coming. But what about in between? Why were we left here?

Salvation has three tenses to it. There is a past: we were saved from the penalty of sin; that happened at the cross. We will be saved from the ongoing presence of sin; that will happen at the coming of Christ, or when we go to be with Him. But there's a third dimension—not only the past, not only the future, but the present. We are being saved from the power of sin. I've got to ask myself, as you have to ask yourself, "Am I making any progress? How long have I known the Lord?"

Faith Has Problems

God allows storms into our lives because you don't develop your faith in the calm. You develop your faith in the crises. You develop your faith when you have no other way to look but up to the only worthy object of faith.

And so, we come to lesson number three: biblical faith has problems. Oops! Really? Yes. A Christian is not a person without problems. A Christian is a person who has the problem solver living within. I've been through the entire Bible I don't know how many times, and I cannot find one verse of scripture that promises you exemption from problems. Enablement — plenty of verses. But not exemption.

I happen to believe that there is no growth without tension. That's why Paul says in 1 Corinthians 10:13 (KJV), *"There hath no testing taken you, but such as is common to man."* It's not unique to you that you have difficulties in your marriage, that you have problems with your temper, that you have whatever you have. These are common to all people.

> *"We are all faced with a series of great opportunities*
>
> *Brilliantly disguised as impossible situations."*
>
> — *Chuck Swindoll*

"But God is faithful," continues Paul, "who will not allow you to be tested above what you are able, but who will with the testing provide a way of escape that you may be able to bear it." The ultimate test is this: are you going to hold up or fold up? James puts it this way, *"Count it all joy when you fall into various trials."* (James 1:2, NKJV). By the way, did you notice? He says, "Count it all joy when," not if.

Peter says, *"Think it not strange concerning the fiery trial which is to try you as though some strange thing happened to you."* (1 Peter 4:12, KJV)

You say, "Well, great, I don't have any problems now."

Well, be patient. They're on their way.

What do we often do? You get down and say, "O Lord, make me like your Son."

And the moment He goes to work, you say, "Lord, what happened?"

"It's nothing. I'm just answering your prayer."

Remember that Jesus Christ, although he was God's Son, "yet learned obedience." How? By the things that He suffered (Hebrews 5:8).

> "It's in going through the process
>
> That a man becomes processed."
>
> — *Bishop Joel Njoku*

Look to God

One of my favorite Old Testament stories is found in Numbers 13. The children of Israel were wending their way through the wilderness, and they came to a place called Kadesh, in the desert of Paran, just a wide spot in the road except for a decision they made there, a decision that determined their destiny. God had told them to go directly into the land. They said, in effect, "Hey, let's not play the part of a fool. Let's appoint a committee." So, in typical committee fashion, they come back with a majority and a minority report.

The majority says, "Man, we can't go up there. There are giants in the land. Besides, we're just a collection of grasshoppers."

> "If you can find a path with no obstacles,
>
> It probably doesn't lead anywhere."
>
> — *Frank A. Clark*

But there are two men that bring back the minority report. Do you remember their names? Joshua and Caleb. Can you remember the names of any of the other ten men? Most likely not. Yet they're all found in the opening verses of Numbers 13. We say the majority is always right. Really? In this case, the majority was flat wrong. And it was as a result of a majority decision that an entire generation perished in the wilderness. The only guys who ever did get into the land were Joshua and Caleb.

Now what's the difference between Joshua and Caleb and the other guys? You think Joshua went in and said, "Caleb, I don't see any giants in the land. Do you?" I think the guy had 20/20 vision. I think if CBC had been on hand to interview them and said, "Who are you?" they'd say "God's grasshoppers reporting for duty." The difference is this: they also saw God.

> *"It's worth taking a risk when*
>
> *Motivated by faith in God's word."*
>
> *— Ruben Barreto*

What do you see? You've got problems with your kids? You've got problems down at the office? You've got problems in a marriage? You wonder how long it will last. The ultimate issue is not whether you have problems but whether you know anyone who can do anything about them. Who is your focus?

Learn to Trust God, Not Yourself

Trusting God is simply believing that He loves you, He's good, He has the power to help you, He wants to help you, and He will help you. Christians are called believers, but many times, we are more like unbelieving believers. We trust our friends, the bank, the stock market, or the government more than we trust God and His word.

> *"Faith is not the power of positive thinking;*
>
> *It is believing in God and trusting that*
>
> *His will is always best even when you cannot understand why."*
>
> — **Shari Howerton**

In John 15:5, Jesus says that apart from Him, we can do nothing. We need to lean on him for help with everything in our lives. Sadly, a lot of people go to church, hear what they should do and then go home and try to do it on their own. They usually end up desperately telling God how hard they're trying to do what they need to do, and they're leaving Him out! God wants us to put Him first in our lives. He wants us to put our confidence and trust in Him, all the time, in everything.

Proverbs 3:5-6 says, *"Trust in the Lord with all your heart, and lean not on your own understanding; in all your ways acknowledge him, and He shall direct your paths"* (NKJV). When you accept Jesus Christ as your Savior, the Spirit of God comes to live inside you. This is one of the greatest blessings of salvation: you don't have to go through someone else to get to God. He dwells in your heart and you can learn to hear His voice.

> *"Faith is like Wi-Fi. It's invisible, but it has the power*
>
> *To connect you to what you need."*
>
> — **Abel Damina**

The best way to hear from God and know how He wants you to live is to know what the Bible, His word, says. God's word gives us wisdom. And as we study the Bible, our mind is renewed so we no longer just think the way the world thinks; we can think the way God thinks!

We must habitually study the word to really have confidence in God and know we can hear Him. The Bible is food for our spirit. As we spend time reading and meditating on scripture, we develop a strong spirit. Then we can hear God speaking to our heart where He dwells in us and we make decisions based upon what He's leading us to do, not just what we may think, feel or want.

When you go beyond what you want, what you think and what you feel, and do what the word and the spirit of God tell you to do, you can develop good habits and break bad ones. You come to a place where the blessings of God — His righteousness, peace and joy — overflow in your life.

Life is simple and peaceful when we come to God like little children and say, "God, I don't want to live on my own. I want to trust you. When I don't know what to do, I'll trust you. When I don't understand why, I'll trust you. I'll do my part with your help, and when I'm done, I'll trust you to do the rest."

"Faith is taking the first step even when

You don't see the whole staircase."

— Martin Luther King Jr.

Jesus experienced hard times too...the road to the cross was no small matter. But He had to decide to go through it. He even asked God if it was necessary (but we know how this amazing love story ended). Just like Jesus had to make a choice, you and I also must decide to go through hard times.

In good times it's easy to talk about faith. It's easy to see why we believe and encourage others to "keep the faith" when they're feeling down. But what about periods of prolonged suffering or surprise attacks?

> *"Your faith can move mountains*
>
> *And your doubt can create them."*
>
> — *Bishop Harry Jackson*

Keeping Faith

Our faith isn't always tested in the good times; our faith is tested during trials and times of challenge. When we ask, "Where are you, God?" and hear crickets chirping, that's when we're left to decide. Will we believe anyway — cultivating a more mature faith? Or will we decide He's not there, falling back on all the voices we've heard in the past?

Have the God kind of faith. Sometimes we can see the temptation at work in these moments; sometimes we can't. We take forward steps and backward steps (and side steps and missteps), but we're growing when our number of forward steps become greater. Taking that forward step is your faith in action.

> *"Faith is seeing light with your heart*
>
> *When all your eyes see is darkness."*
>
> — *Barbara Johnson*

Choose to remain faithful when there is no visible finish line and no feeling of relief. Lean into it and bear through the discomfort that comes from trusting in what you cannot see. It's not taking a risk, it's strengthening your faith. Are you struggling with trusting God? Think of a yoga stretch or new skill; getting to the next level requires a time of discomfort while pushing forward. You will feel (and eventually see) the difference. *"This calls for patient endurance on the part of the saints who obey God's commandments and remain faithful to Jesus."* (Revelation 14:12, NIV)

During the discomfort, pray that God guides your steps and keeps you strong. Temptation will sway in and out to mislead and falsely appease you but pray right through it. *"Watch and pray, so that you will not fall into temptation. The spirit is willing, but the body is weak."* (Matthew 26:41, NIV) and if you fall for it… which we all do at times… start again. Keep choosing God over and over and over.

> *"You can never cross the ocean until you have the courage*
>
> *To lose sight of the shore."*
>
> — ***Christopher Columbus***

When you feel the struggle heavy on your back, bury yourself in more good soil. Surround yourself with loving friends, pop into a church before starting the day, read the Bible, put some encouraging messages where you can see them, attend a service, watch an online sermon, ask someone you love to pray with you, or meditate on positive thoughts. My mother always tells me, son, stay in the word. The tough times will hit you, but we are living for something bigger.

The Only One You Can Trust

All things do work together for our good! This is a key scripture for Christians when we go through hard or disappointing times. When something doesn't happen the way we would like it to happen, we can believe God will work things out for good. It's the place we can always come back to in every kind of trial. Now this doesn't mean the trials are necessarily good, but God can work them out for our good because He is awesome.

If we love God and really want His will for our life, I think it's safe to say that we can trust Him to bring good from it no matter what happens to us. Even if we must take detours because of our own stupidity or if we're innocent but someone else gets involved and brings hurt and pain into our life, we can trust God to work it out. I like to say, "No person on earth and no devil in hell can keep me from God's will."

> "All that grace has provided,
>
> We need faith to receive."
>
> — **Great Igwe**

We only seem to really grow during hard times. I think it's because it's during those times that we really press into God and go to a deeper level in our relationship with Him. Why? Because we must. It's our only choice if we want to make it through the difficulty. When we trust God, He gives us the comfort of knowing that He can work bad things out for our good.

> "As long as your eye is consistently fixed on Jesus,
>
> Rest assured that you will never sink, and if you do sink,
>
> Rest assured that you will not get drowned."
>
> — *Dr Paul Enenche*

Your will is one of the most powerful things you have. Setbacks are setups in our lives for God to do something greater. With God on your side, you can rest assured that when adversity arises, a new level is on the way. Are you discouraged today because you're facing a difficult battle? We all have things that come against us in life, and we encounter unfair people and situations. But just because you have opposition doesn't mean you're not in God's will. God is in control, and He's directing your steps. What's meant for your harm, God is going to use to your advantage.

"The world says, seeing is believing.

Faith says, believing is seeing."

— **Tim Hall**

Many times, God will speak things that contradict what we see with our eyes. That's why we must walk by faith and not by sight. People may tell you that you'll never get well; circumstances may look like you'll never get out of debt, never meet the right person, or never accomplish your dreams. But if you listen with your spiritual ears, you'll hear a voice saying, "Healing is coming. You will lend and not borrow. New doors are about to open."

"Always remember, you are just one 'hearing'

Away from faith, just one 'knowing' away from peace, and just one 'action' away from total victory."

— **Rex Rouis**

In a drought, God will talk to you about rain. When you're broke, He'll talk to you about abundance. When you feel insignificant, like you'll never make anything out of your life, He'll talk to you about greatness. When you get in agreement with God then you will become what He says about you. You will have what He says you'll have! Many times, God will speak things that contradict what we see with our eyes. That's why we must walk by faith and not by sight. You may feel average today, but 1 John 4:4 says, *"You belong to God."* You are extremely valuable! Learn to recognize your value and how God sees you. You are a child of the highest God!

> *"Faith is God's sovereign stamp of approval upon the things you are hoping for; His presence graced upon your seeking, and His witness placed upon your request."*
>
> — **Rex Rouis**

You can live from a place of peace and rest knowing that God is not only fighting your battles, but He's lined up the exact situations you need in your life to bring you where you're supposed to be. He has the right people that are going to help you already planned out. He has solutions to problems that you can't even see right now. Release your faith and trust Him. His plan is better than yours. You may have situations that don't look like they'll ever change, but God has already arranged good breaks in your future. All it takes is just one touch of God's favor!

If there's anyone who understands heartache and betrayal, it's Joseph. He was betrayed by his brothers, thrown into a pit, and eventually sold into slavery. But all along, God had a plan for Joseph. After his trials, Joseph ended up overseeing all Egypt. He was blessed in such a way that he said in Genesis 41:51 (Amplified Bible, AMP), "God has made me forget all my trouble and hardship." He named his son Manasseh which means in Hebrew "causing to forget."

> *"Most times, great destinies come with great battles. He who desires it, should be prepared for the full package."*
>
> — **Great Igwe**

Like Joseph, God wants to bless you in such a way that you won't remember the pain of the past. You may feel forgotten, but God hasn't forgotten about you. He's seen your heartache and has collected every tear you've shed. He's going to turn your pain around in such a way that you're overwhelmed with His goodness. God is going to cause you to forget!

Nothing has randomly happened in your life. Everything has been carefully orchestrated, the good and the bad, the blessings and the disappointments. Even in times where we've failed and made mistakes, God has already planned how to restore us and get us back on course.

It's easy to judge others, but underneath the dirt, the mess and bad decisions, there's a son or a daughter of the highest God. God is counting on us to represent His love and redemption to those in need. They may be bound on the outside, but like Lazarus, on the inside they're a person of destiny. They just need someone to help remove the grave clothes. Will you be that person? Take time to make a difference in the lives of those who desperately need it.

"Success is to be measured not so much by the position that one has reached in life but by the obstacles which he has overcome to get there."

— *Booker T. Washington*

Are you ready to give up on what you're believing for because all you've heard is no? Well, it's time to get ready because yes is coming! No matter who has said no or how many times a door has closed, God has already set a date to bring His promises to pass in your life. But there is one thing God needs from you, and that is your yes. Allow Him to teach you how to be determined in your faith like never before. Your faith will grow as you hear amazing stories from the Bible of men and women who dared to believe God for a yes and saw amazing breakthroughs.

Whether you're battling an enemy of sickness, depression, fear, lack or struggle — get ready, God is about to judge in your favor. What has stopped you in the past is going to stop you no more. Let this book help you step into a new level of destiny and wholeness as you break past barriers with God's help. Do you feel stuck or restricted today because of a past mistake, an addiction, a health matter you're desperate to see change, or a situation you can't control? We all face limiting situations, but the good news is that God can overturn areas where we feel blocked from moving forward and living our fullest lives.

"Strength does not come from winning. Your struggles develop your strengths. When you go through hardships and decide not to surrender, that is true strength."

— Arnold Schwarzenegger

What is it that you want to accomplish? Proverbs 16:3 (NIV) says, *"Commit to the LORD whatever you do, and he will establish your plans."* You can't do it on your own, but you're not on your own. You can commit those important things in your life to the God who is committed to you! He is saying, "Focus on your commitments and believe that I'm going to help you bring them to pass." You must put your plans into action if God is going to help you.

It's easy to believe we have favor when good things are happening, but you can have favor even in the challenge. God will cause you to succeed in the middle of trouble. He's not limited by our conditions; He's limited by our faith and thinking. God is at work in your life and has a plan, His divine plan to reveal His incredible favor and goodness in your life. But, you must do your part and trust in God's timing and plan. Release your faith, raise your expectancy and watch how God will miraculously turn your darkest hour into your greatest hour as the odds are shifted in your favor.

"You can't change the direction of the wind, but you can adjust your sails to always reach your desired destination."

— Jimmy Dean

Do you feel like the odds are against you today? Maybe you're facing a difficult situation that doesn't look like it will ever get any better. Or, you've prayed diligently for God to answer a specific prayer, but nothing is happening. I have good news for you. There is light coming your way.

Chapter Six

RISE UP AND FIGHT

No one said life was meant to be easy. If yours is harder than most, you will have to fight harder than most. No one is given an easy path; only some are prepared to fight their battles. Are you ready to rise and fight?

"No pressure, no diamonds."

— *Thomas Carlyle*

It's easy to feel destroyed, empty, defeated, and overcome. It's easy to pass the blame, but real victors are the ones who despite their predicament, despite their limitations, decided never to give in. It is not over yet. If you still breathe then there is hope.

Today the battle of your life may present itself! Are you prepared for the battles ahead? Are you prepared to win? You fight for your family! Don't allow that cancer take you so easily, don't allow that sickness knock you down. You reach. You claw. You hold on. Today is a battle. Tomorrow is a victory lap.

> *"Sometimes in tragedy we find our life's purpose –*
>
> *The eye sheds a tear to find its focus."*
>
> — **Bishop Harry Jackson Jr**

What happened to that survival instinct you were born with? Kicking and screaming your way into the world. Fighting for one breath of air! Fighting for life! We get beaten down so many times along the way, we forget to kick and scream. We forget how hard we fought for that first breath. We forget how to fight back! What if you awoke in the middle of the night to the terrified screams of your family, would you hide in the shadows and hope for the best, or would you attack with such ferocity the devil himself would cower in fear?

That's how you attack every day, fighting to take your life back! Because you were born a lion! And don't you dare let any sheep convince you otherwise. Tear any man limb from limb that tries to put you back in that cage. You rip him to shreds! No one will deny you, no one will stop you. Be like a wild animal with one last chance to make it. Whatever it takes, to get back to where you belong. At the top of the food chain.

"Just because fate doesn't deal you the right cards, doesn't mean you should give up. It just means you have to play the cards you have to their maximum potential." — **Les Brown**

Today is the day, now is the time! Stand up and you stand tall! Because you know you can achieve anything you put your mind to. Don't sit back and watch the enemy take what's yours! Your joy, dreams, goals, vision, marriage, and your life. Don't allow the enemy steal your man, your wife and destroy your relationship. Rise and fight. Show no mercy! Take the game and shove it right back in their face! Let them watch in awe, as you smash through your plateaus and obliterate their records! Work until you have nothing left, and then go again & again!

If you can breathe you have opportunity, seize that opportunity! Don't you grow old and gray begging for one more chance. This is the time. It's either now or never. Stop the blame game. Everyone has brick walls in their way! Real men of steel are forged in adversity. You will slash through any obstacle. You don't sleep until you've done all you can to be one step closer to where you belong.

> *"Being challenged in life is inevitable,*
>
> *Being defeated is optional."*
>
> **— Roger Crawford**

Whatever your battle, you fight to win! It's all you got! Leave no stone unturned. Leave nothing on the table. Not an ounce of effort left in your body. If you must die striving for it, you will die a legend! You will die with honor! If you die with no regrets, you will die in peace.

Fight Back: Disappoint Their Intentions toward You

I know some of you are tired of being victims. Tired of being told that you can't achieve your dreams. You won't achieve your goals. That the things in life you want to do, you can't do. That the things you want in life are unreachable. I know you are tired of hearing that. That is why I am talking to you today through this book. Because today I want you to fight back for what you believe in. Fight back for what you want to achieve, fight for your dreams, fight for your goals.

> *"Success introduces you to the world,*
>
> *But adversity introduces you to yourself."*
>
> **— Bishop David Oyedepo**

Never allow your circumstances rob you of your willpower because you are stronger than you know, more capable than they think. You are so endowed with greatness and strength that it will take more than an amputated leg, sickness, betrayal, divorce, or the death of a loved one to put you down. Rise and fight.

Sometimes you're not just fighting for yourself. Sometimes you're fighting for your friends, your children, spouse, or entire family! The bottom line is making certain you fight back! Not with guns, sword, or evil but with your mind. Your enthusiasm, your determination, and your attitude.

Yes, I know! They told you that you can't do this. You might as well give up. You will never achieve what you set out to achieve. Well, that's the thing about greatness, about being a champion. No one expected you to make it, but you go out and do it anyway. Prove them wrong. Prove them wrong! Greatness is not just about the money, it's about the achievements. It's about doing something that others doubted. It's about listening to the doubters, then making them eat their own words.

You Can Do It

I guarantee you can do it. If you put 100% in. Today is the day you do it! Today is the day you succeed! Today is the day you prevail! Today is the day you walk over your enemies. He thought you couldn't live without him, they thought you would never grow out of this predicament, but they were wrong. Today decide to get up, shake off the past, the hurt, the limitation, and confront your future like a lion with boldness. This is the day you make destiny count.

> "Though no one can go back and make a brand-new start, anyone can start from now and make a brand-new ending." — **Carl Bard**

Let go of the bitterness, let go of the past, embrace the situation. Walk up to the mirror and tell that person staring at you in the mirror that this is not the end. You can make it. You can still thrive; you can succeed no matter the limitations. Rise up to the challenge. You did not bargain for this, you had no control over its existence but you sure have control of how you will live it.

Where you become that person that others can look to and say, he/she went through it, so I can do it! We feed off each other and we look up to someone that's great like they're special. But they're just like you. The only difference is that they decided to fight, to thrive, and to succeed no matter what. They decided nothing can stop them from becoming the person they desire to become. Not the wheelchair, not education, not divorce, or death, or sickness. You've got that greatness inside of you!

"There are no great men, there are

Only great challenges,

Which ordinary men like you and me are forced by circumstances to meet?"

— **William Frederick Halsey**

So, get that greatness that's been in you all along, to come out. And the only way to do it, is to take one step. You take one step towards your goal. You take one step toward your dream. Take one step in the forward direction. Make sure, in everything you do, you are trying to reach greatness. You are trying to beat the odds. You are trying to succeed. You are putting your best foot forward.

Every day! Not just today but every day. Fight back every day. Today, and every other day, because it is the little effort you put in every day, the little fire you light every day, that little step and determination, that create the big picture. I tell you, nothing beats character, and nothing beats hard work. Not today, not any other day.

> "No one is going to hand me success. I must go out and get it myself. That's why I'm here. To dominate. To conquer. Both the world, and myself."
>
> — *Lewis Howes*

It's time to take responsibility for your life. It's time for the next level! It's time to rise to your true potential! My commitment and obsession is always to be better today than I was yesterday. If I must make sacrifices to do that: so be it. If I must tell that person I can't go out drinking with him anymore: so it is. Because that's not what I value.

> "Life's challenges are not supposed to paralyze you,
>
> They're supposed to help you discover who you are."
>
> — *Bernice Johnson*

Anything or anyone that is taking me further away from my dreams must go. I'm committed to self-development not self-destruction, and you know, any person that is meant to be with me on the journey, will choose that higher road with me. Yes, a tougher road, but it is also a much more rewarding one.

I want my life to mean something. To be able to look back at my life and say, yeah, I made some tough decisions, but they were the right decisions. So many people don't get it. They piss their life away every weekend for what? So, they can complain about their current circumstances for the rest of the week?

No chance! I'm in charge of my own life! It's all on me! I take responsibility. I act. And I get it done! You will never hear me complain about another person or circumstance as the reason I'm not where I want to be. I am a perfect reflection of the hard work or lack of work I put in. And luck, that only comes to those who have paid their dues. If I am weak in a certain area, it won't be for long.

Because I'm committed to be better. I will learn, I will read. I will make it happen. I will find a way. I will work until that weakness is turned into strength. No one can beat me, because I don't give up! I'm relentless. You might knock me down, but I never stay down! It's time to rise. Rise up to your battles! Rise up past your limitations! Set the standard for those around you! Don't conform to the standard, like a sheep. Get out and lead the way!

Stop the Self-Pity

Not sure if you are living in a state of self-pity? It's time to get honest with you! When you can be honest, you can become aware of how self-pity can really drag you down in life, and you will be more likely to try and overcome it. The truth is that self-pity is addictive. It's like a drug, and soon you barely even notice that you are playing the game of self-pity. In fact, it may make you feel good about yourself at times, especially when it allows you to get attention as well as sympathy from yourself and from other people.

Self-pity is a common response to stressful events. Something bad happens, you feel helpless, and you feel sorry for yourself. That's how things play out. The problem is that throwing a pity party does nothing to improve the stressful event you're facing. Self-pity promotes inaction and acts as a gateway to learned helplessness and depression. The key to avoiding this kind of useless behavior is recognizing the warning signs.

> *"Fear is a habit; so is self-pity, defeat, anxiety, despair, hopelessness and resignation. You can eliminate all these negative habits with two simple resolves: I can, and I will."*
>
> — *Napoleon Hill*

Studies in the *Journal of Personality* show that people who frequently indulge in self-pity see themselves as controlled by both chance and by others they see as more powerful than they are. People who feel sorry for themselves internalize their anger instead of expressing it. They ruminate or obsess over what went wrong and why it's "not fair," instead of acting to make things better. While these thoughts might feel comforting at the time, they lead to bigger problems.

When things go bad, it's easy to feel sorry for yourself. It's easy to ask, "why me?" But there's absolutely no value in this. When you feel self-pity, others don't feel sorry for you. They see you as weak. They resent you and want to either avoid you or crush you completely. The more you feel sorry for yourself in life, the more people will take advantage of you. You'll be taken advantage of over and over until you're swimming in a swamp of self-pity, alone and completely helpless. The only way to avoid this fate is to start standing up for yourself and start channeling your emotions in a more productive manner.

> *"Bad things do happen; how I respond to them defines my character and the quality of my life. I can choose to sit in perpetual sadness, immobilized by the gravity of my loss, or I can choose to rise from the pain and treasure the most precious gift I have - life itself."*
>
> — *Walter Anderson*

Some of us experience more adversity and painful events in our lives than others. We wonder why our difficulties don't happen to the "bad" people out there instead of us. Unfortunately, life is not fair.

Awful things happen. Dreadful circumstances or tragedies will affect most of our lives at some point. It's okay to cry and feel sorry for yourself and your circumstances, mope around, or get angry. But at some point, you must shake it off, let go of the past, and choose to not let it consume you entirely. Otherwise, you won't be able to learn from the experience and move forward in a constructive way.

Now, I am not addressing true clinical depression here. I am talking about self-pity, defined by Merriam-Webster dictionary as "a self-indulgent dwelling on your own sorrows or misfortunes."

"Self-pity is a sinkhole from which no rescuing hand can drag

You because you have chosen to sink."

— *Elisabeth Elliot*

Discovering that we chronically self-pity and taking steps to overcome this issue is part of the evolutionary process of self-transformation which stems from an understanding and acceptance of ourselves. So, if you suspect that you constantly self-pity, don't fight it. Don't hide from it in shame or embarrassment. Rather, face it, and accept it as a fact of your life. Embrace the fact that you are flawed and fallible ... just like everyone else. Only then can you hope to make long-lasting changes within yourself.

Self-pity is a Choice

When we fall into the depression of self-pity, we allow it to take control of our lives. We become completely self-absorbed. It is destructive to dwell on negative events and carry that bitterness and resentment forward. When we keep our focus on the hurt, we aren't focused on taking control of our lives. If we blame negative circumstances for our place in life, we are giving up responsibility and control. We whine and feel sorry for ourselves. We can choose to spread our misery, or we can choose to rise above our circumstances. Self-pity is a form of selfishness. It makes us less aware of the needs and suffering of others. Our own suffering is all we think or care about in our self-absorbed state.

> *"You can never win when*
>
> *You wear the ugly cloak of self-pity*
>
> *And the sour sound of whining."*
>
> — **Og Mandino**

Whether you've been rejected by a love interest or you're overwhelmed by a looming deadline, throwing a pity party won't help. In fact, feeling sorry for yourself can be downright self-destructive. It makes overcoming adversity difficult—if not impossible—and it keeps you stuck. Mentally strong people refuse to allow self-pity to sabotage their goals. Instead, they use life's inevitable hardships to grow stronger and become better. Here are 6 ways they avoid the trap:

1. They face their feelings

Mentally strong people allow themselves to experience emotions like grief, disappointment, and loneliness head-on. They do not distract themselves from uncomfortable emotions by questioning whether their problems are "fair," or by convincing themselves they've suffered more than those around them. They know the best way to deal with discomfort is to just get through it.

2. They recognize warning signs of the downward spiral

When you focus on everything that is going wrong, your thoughts become exaggeratedly negative, and those thoughts will negatively affect your behavior if you dwell on them. The combination of negative thinking and inactivity fuels further feelings of self-pity. Mentally strong people recognize when they are at risk of becoming caught in a downward spiral and act to prevent themselves from living a pitiful life.

3. They question their perceptions

Our emotional state influences how we perceive reality. When you feel sorry for yourself, you likely focus on the bad things going on in your life, while overlooking the good. Mentally strong people question whether their thoughts represent reality. They ask themselves questions like, "Is my luck always bad?" Or, "is my entire life really ruined?" Such questions allow them to recognize when their outlook isn't realistic, and to create a more realistic perception of their situation.

4. They turn their negative thoughts into behavioral experiments

Successful people don't allow negative thoughts to turn into self-fulfilling prophecies; they perform behavioral experiments to prove those thoughts wrong. When they find themselves thinking things like, "I could never put on a presentation as good as this one," they respond with, "challenge accepted!"

5. They reserve their resources for productive activities

Every minute you dwell on self-pity is 60 seconds you delay working on a solution to your problems. Mentally strong people refuse to waste precious time and energy on their misery. Instead, they devote their finite resources to productive activities that can improve the situation.

6. They practice gratitude

It's hard to feel self-pity and gratitude at the same time. Self-pity is about thinking, "I deserve better", while gratitude is about thinking, "I have more than I need." Mentally strong people recognize all that they must be grateful for in life right down to the fresh air to breathe and clean water to drink.

You can choose to lift yourself up and enjoy life! You oversee your own happiness. It is your personal responsibility. So, go ahead and cry and mope and feel sorry for yourself and stay in bed all day. Feel the pain and the hurt. Live your reality and misery. It's okay and even healthy to do that. But then let it go!

Don't let it consume your life. You are not alone or unloved. Remember there are other people in your life who need you. There are people you haven't even met yet who need you! You can't help anyone else if you only see yourself. You cannot change the past, but you can change your future.

This is Not the End: Kick out Depression

I want you to know that, no matter where you are in life… no matter how low you have sunk…no matter how bleak your situation… this is not the end. This is not the end of your story. This is not the final chapter of your life. I know it may be hard right now. But if you just hang in there, stick it out, you will find that this tough moment will pass, and, if you are committed to using this pain, using it to build your character, finding a greater meaning for the pain, you will find that, in time, you can turn your life around, and help others going through the same struggles.

The world right now is in the middle of a mental health crisis. It's estimated almost half the population suffers from depression at some stage throughout their life. Rather than join the queue, it's important we learn why we get down, and then how we can change it, because believe it or not, we create our own negative feelings and we can also ensure that we turn our lives around and be a positive change for others.

The reason anyone gets depressed always comes down to the consistent thoughts we think, and the consistent beliefs we hold. If I believe I am fat, horrible, ugly and unworthy of love, I will most likely become depressed or have depressive thoughts. If my thought process is "I must be in a relationship and earn x amount to be happy" I might become depressed if I don't achieve those goals.

The point here is that anyone that is depressed is so, because there is an external factor that didn't materialize in their life i.e. (they have lost something outside of their control, or don't have something that is out of their control). Again, I'm not referring to clinical depression here.

The most common reasons for depression are: job loss, relationship break downs or nonexistence, body image, and comparison to others. The only way out of this is to work on you, every day. In school we are taught how to get a job, but no one teaches us how to live in a state of happiness. No one teaches us how important our conscious and unconscious thoughts and associations are. Is our happiness not worth more than a job? Yes, it is.

HJAnd before you say, happiness won't pay my bills – happiness will pay your bills, when you realize you will be 10 times more energized, focused, and take positive action in your life, when you first choose to develop yourself as a priority, and then get to all the "stuff" of the world.

I've seen some people, who many would consider to "have it all" end their life because they thought they were not good enough. A thought, a belief within them told them they were not worthy. These people that many were jealous of, even envious of, felt they were not good enough. On June 8, 2018, Anthony Bourdain, the TV celebrity and food writer who hosted CNN'S *Parts Unknown*, was found dead in his hotel room.

He was in France working on his series on culinary traditions around the world. Bourdain was 61. CNN confirmed the death, saying that Bourdain was found unresponsive that Friday morning by friend and Chef Eric Ripert near the French city of Strasbourg. They called his death a suicide. I wonder what would make such a high achieving, well to do man with all his connections and immunities decide to take his own life, leaving behind all he has worked for. The big pay check, cars, houses and above all, a lovely daughter.

The people you envy sometimes wish they have your kind of life.

You must value yourself enough, to take the time every single day to work on you. To engage in something that will ensure you are a positive influence on the world. This of course doesn't mean life will suddenly be perfect. The same life-challenges will show up, but if your mind is strong, if you mind is at peace, your reaction to the challenging times will be very different. Your reaction will be "How can I make this work?" not "Why is this happening to me?"

And then others will look to you, not with pity but with hope, because your strength will become their hope, their strength. You really can be that powerful. You can ditch the victim story; you can leave the pain behind and focus on how you will react next. How you will react positively.

Read. Read all you can read to get your mind in a positive place. Take steps to ensure you will be in a better position next time. Whatever pain you are suffering, how can you ensure it won't show again? Take little steps, and soon you will be at the top of the staircase. You are more than worthy! You deserve to experience how great life can be – and you owe it to the world to be that positive change for others. To inspire others who will look to you and say, he/she did it, and I can do it.

Chapter Seven

RISE UP AND FACE YOUR FEAR

F. E. A. R: false evidence appearing real.

Underneath your fears lie great opportunities. Because when you start doing the things that scare you the most, tearing down the invisible barriers that separate you from the good life, you become the person you've always dreamed about in your mind: your ideal self. That means finding your courage is a life-changing decision. Fear will always be around to tell you what you can't do—it's up to you to face your fears and tell yourself that you can.

> *"If you are distressed by anything external,*
>
> *The pain is not due to the thing itself,*
>
> *But to your estimate of it; and this you have*
>
> *The power to revoke at any moment."*
>
> *— Marcus Aurelius*

Throughout this world there live only two kinds of people: those who have conquered their fears, and those who are living their fears. Those who are living their fears and those who are living their dreams because they had the courage to take on their fears. Rise above your fear. Embrace it and then turn it into your motivation. Let your passion to succeed be greater than your fear and you will break down mountains and fill up valleys along your paths to greatness.

What is the number one killer of dreams? What do you think is the number one reason the majority fail to live a life that they want to live? What is the number one reason why people fail to succeed... at any level? It's not luck. It's not lack of money or opportunity. It's certainly not circumstance. It's fear.

> *"Living with fear stops us taking risks, and if you don't go out on the branch, you're never going to get the best fruit."*
>
> *— Sarah Parish*

Fear is the greatest killer of dreams that ever roamed planet earth. Fear is that voice inside you that says you can't. The voice that gets louder and stronger every time you listen. Every time you let fear dictate your decision, fear grows stronger. Fear grows bigger. Fear is the voice of average. The voice of the settler. If you must walk tall in this tough time you have to deal with this enemy.

The only way you can change is to step right into your fear. You must sum up all the courage inside you and do the thing you fear most. Failure may come. Your greatest fears may be realized. And that is why you go in with the attitude that you will do whatever it takes to conquer that fear. No matter how many times I fail, no matter how many times I feel rejected, embarrassed, down, out, I will not give up! I will keep at it until my greatest fear dies! I will stand toe to toe with fear!

My largest fear carries my greatest growth. I will never let my fears decide my fate; I am bigger than any fear. Fear has no place within my heart. Fear is conditioned into us from a young age. Many don't pay attention to the stages of fear.

"Be careful."

"You can't do that."

"Play it safe."

These consistent fearful thoughts add up, live inside us and form our psychology, which, for most turns into inaction. For most turns into average. For most turns into settling for a life they aren't passionate about living. It's time to take back control! So how do we overcome our fear? Find something that is more painful than your fear.

"Inaction breeds doubt and fear. Action breeds confidence and courage.

If you want to conquer fear, do not sit home and think about it.

Go out and get busy."

— Dale Carnegie

If you have a fear of failure that is stopping you from going all out and achieving at a high level, a more painful thought might be disappointing your family or the thought of your kids seeing you settle for a life you don't want and knowing they will follow in your footsteps. Maybe a greater pain would be the thought of getting to the end of your life and knowing you never really lived, you just existed. You got by. I need you to really feel that pain. Think about it. Feel a deep emotional connection to the pain.

> *"One of the greatest discoveries a man makes, one of his great surprises,*
>
> *Is to find he can do what he was afraid he couldn't do."*
>
> *— Henry Ford*

Write down why you won't settle for that pain anymore. Write down why you must conquer this fear once and for all. What would be worse than your fear? They say if you have a strong enough why, the how will come, the results will come. Why must you do this? Be more fearful of what it will cost you if you don't do it! Be more fearful of the impact it will have on your future if you don't act. Be more fearful of how it will impact the lives of your loved ones if you don't act.

> *"Have the courage to go after your dreams,*
>
> *Or live with regrets for not doing so."*
>
> *— Barack Obama*

What would you do, if you had no fear of failure? Why are you waiting? Everyone has something they fear doing, that, if they did it, if they conquered the fear, would have a huge impact on their life. Maybe it's the fear of failure. Maybe they fear embarrassment or rejection if it doesn't work out. Maybe they fear starting that business.

Making that call. That one thing you know you must do and if you do it, it will change your life forever. The greatest success in your life is waiting for you, right after you conquer your greatest fears. Everything you want in life is on the other side of fear. It is impossible to reach your true potential if you don't face your greatest fears… that is just common sense. The thing that makes you uncomfortable, but you know would make you stronger and better if you did it. That's the thing you must face. That is the thing you must conquer if you want your freedom. The greatest success in your life is waiting for you, right after you conquer your greatest fears.

"One fear conquered is two battles won already."

— Great Igwe

Fear induces one of two responses. We must either forget everything and run, or face everything and rise. Simplifying our experiences to just fighting or running only touches on the surface. There is much more involved, or rather there is much more that needs to be involved when dealing with a frightening situation.

Because so few people understand what implications the simplest of decisions have on their psyche, few bother to follow through properly. If you decide to get yourself out of a dangerous or frightening situation, then you can't simply run and hope for the best.

Your cognitive abilities are too highly developed to allow you to simply go on living like nothing happened. Something did happen and the more difficult the decision to call it quits was, the more profound and lasting the effect it will have on you. If you're going to run, then you must actively forget about the situation you were in. You can't simply go on living your life the way you were living it before because it will all catch up with you sooner or later.

> "I learned that courage was not the absence of fear,
> But the triumph over it. The brave man is not he who does not feel afraid,
> But he who conquers that fear."
>
> — *Nelson Mandela*

The only way to truly forget is to delve deeper into the problem, dissecting it to the point where you understand that the issue no longer requires or is deserving of your attention. Most will call this closure. Deciding to run and call it quits, in any of the most important facets of life, is a difficult decision to make and an even more difficult decision to live with. If you react to your fear by running then don't just brush the situation off, do your best to understand why the decision you made was the right one.

Get that much needed closure so that you can focus your thoughts on the present and future. If you now regret the decision to run, then dissect the matter until you understand why it was a bad decision and why you will never make that same decision again. Once you understand, forget and move on.

> "To escape fear, you must go through it,
> Not around it."
>
> — *Richie Norton*

On the other hand, if fear triggers the fighting response in you then be sure you know exactly what you are getting yourself into. If you decide to fight, then you must fight to win. You must face everything fighting against you and rise above it all. If you are going to fight, then fight to kill. Most people fail in life because they make decisions they cannot follow through with. They respond to fear, aggressively for example, but then fear the decision they made and end up failing miserably.

"It is not the things we see that birth fear;

What births fear is our perception of the thing."

— Great Igwe

If you decide to fight, then be sure that you are ready to fight. Be sure that you are willing to do what needs to be done no matter how difficult or scary it may be. If you get in the ring, then fight until you either rise above everything and everyone else or until you are torn to pieces. If you're going to fight, then fight until the end; fight to come out on top. You're already lucky because you're human. Make that mean something.

Fear is a made-up concept, it doesn't exist. Think about it. Say you fear failure. You really fear a possibility. A thought in your head about something that may (or may not) occur in the future. It's not real. It's your imagination. Your thoughts do nothing to empower you. Let go of that fear and focus on what steps you can take to get to the place you want to get to. What is that one thing you must do, that could change everything in your life? Remember you cannot be a sheep and expect to eat the lion share. No way. If you must eat the lion share you have to become a lion. Bold, courageous and above all resilient.

Get Out of Your Comfort Zone

Your comfort zone is your enemy. One of the biggest ironies I can think of, is when you live life trying to stay comfortable, life will send you more and more discomfort. It's true; life will send you more and more problems.

Life will keep throwing rocks at you. Life will keep handing you resistance, struggles, issues. And because people are so concerned about staying comfortable instead of growing and reaching higher, because people don't want to address their limitations and move beyond them, they keep struggling.

Many has failed a lot of times that they become too afraid to try again because they are afraid they will fail again. This happens even to the best of us. You have written the examination four times and failed four times, you have been in several relationship that you gave your best to it and yet all of them ended up being a disaster and now you are afraid to open up and love again because you are afraid it will end up the same manner.

Maybe yours is a business idea you are trying to bring to limelight but despite all your effort, nothing seem to change making afraid of even trying again. But it's time you give it another try, open your heart again for love, give that exam one more try, give that business one more push, show up one more time, make that phone call one more time. Send in that application or resume just one more time. Give your spouse one more chance and I bet you be surprise at the outcome you will get. You can still experience happiness and breakthrough. It is not over yet.

"One isn't necessarily born with courage, but one is born with potential. Without courage, we cannot practice any other virtue with consistency. We can't be kind, true, merciful, generous, or honest."

— *Maya Angelou*

Listen, you are not here on this planet to sip apple martinis on the beach and get yourself a tan. You are here to grow. And if you won't make yourself uncomfortable life will give you plenty of reasons to push you out of your comfort zone. So, you have one of two options. Either you commit to constant growth and feeling discomfort upon your own accord and you become the master of your own destiny, or you hand over the keys and you let life happen to you by default.

One path leads you to success and the other path leads you to constant struggle and pain. It's your choice. Do you think Steve Jobs started Apple feeling comfortable about it? Do you think top athletes sleep their way to high performance? Do you think Oscar winning actors procrastinated their way to high achievement? No. So why are you giving in to wasting time with Netflix marathons? And to chronic procrastination?

> *"The best way out is always through."*
>
> *— Robert Frost*

Why are you running to the bar the second your best friend texts you to come out? You have got to be willing to make the hard decision. You've got to be willing to feel uncomfortable. To feel awkward, to face rejection, to fail, to feel pressure. You've got to be willing to face those things, because that's what's necessary for you to grow.

How many times have you looked at your life and said "man, if I only knew then what I know now, I would live my life so differently"? So, is it not possible then, that the life you are living now, you would be living differently, if you began to develop an awareness that you do not currently have?

> *"Only be you strong, and very courageous...*
>
> *Then you will make your way prosperous,*
>
> *And then you will have good success."*
>
> *—Joshua 1:7, 8*

Well guess what? The only way for you to develop knowledge and awareness is to try things you have not yet tried. To do things you have not yet done, to create things you have not yet created, to go to places you have not yet explored.

That is how you grow! That is how you become the person who is worthy of sitting on the beach with their favorite drink. Life rewards you with those experiences after you do the work. There is a real price to success, and life collects the payments, and let me tell you something, life does not accept payment plans.

Life does not let you get away with experiencing things you have not yet earned. Your sacrifice must be paid upfront and in full, and that is the only way you are going to achieve the life you want. So, I strongly suggest that you begin to pay with your discomfort.

"If you want something you've never had,

Then you've got to do something you've never done

Because in the end we regret the chances we didn't take."

— **Abel Damina**

I strongly suggest you start making those calls, that you start approaching that person, that you start practicing kindness and compassion over jealousy and greed, that you confront your anxiety, that you hit the gym, that you study harder, that you jump higher, that you begin waking up early, even if you're not a morning person, that you destroy your procrastination.

That you start doing the things that you know within your heart, you should have started doing a long time ago, so you can start to build the experiences and the knowledge that you need to succeed. That is what I suggest to you. It's time for you to get uncomfortable, it's time for you to start dreaming again, and start going after what was always yours, but what you've ignored for far too long.

> *"The hardest thing to do is leaving your comfort zone.*
>
> *But you must let go of the life you're familiar with*
>
> *And take the risk to live the life you dream about."*
>
> — *T. Arigo*

I promise, when you push yourself into discomfort, your friends will take notice, your colleagues will take notice, your family will take notice, life will take notice, and life will begin to back you up. Life will begin to support you and open doors for you and introduce you to the people who will take you to the next level, but you have got to take the first step!

So, take it. Take it and watch your life explode into greatness. Watch new levels of the game unfold for you. Watch yourself develop into the person who you have always wanted to become. It's all waiting for you outside of your comfort zone. Go for the bigger, smarter, and more courageous you. Step up and step out and face your destiny with boldness. Write your own story. Look beyond the limitation, the singleness, look beyond the betrayal, look beyond the bankruptcy. It's time to leave the shore and dive into the deep. This is your life, this is your time.

> *"Most times the greatness and change we want to see,*
>
> *Are not found by the shore. You must dive into the deep.*
>
> *That is where heroes are made."*
>
> *— Great Igwe*

Take Responsibility for Your Life

If you don't accept full responsibility for your life, no resolution, goal, or dream will save you. You must take full responsibility for the good that arrives, as well as the ugly and inconvenient. Don't be the type to play the blame game, to play victim, "bad things always happen to me" or "I'm not where I want to be because of this person/event."

If you are this type of person, you will never get on in life. Taking responsibility doesn't mean relinquishing control of your life. It means taking control. If someone is stepping over you, if a circumstance keeps pulling you back, be able to see it for what it is! And take massive action to eliminate that person, or thing from your life. It means accepting that you absolutely played a part in all the negatives in your life to this point. Rather than complain and moan about what went wrong, figure out how to fix it.

What can I do now to beat this problem? What can I do now to create a life of success, a life of abundance? What are successful people doing right now and how can I emulate their actions to mirror their success? I guarantee you no successful person is playing the victim role. No human that achieves anything in life plays the blame game. They focus on what they can do now to create a better tomorrow!

> "One of the major tests of maturity, in every aspect of life, spiritual or physical, is a person's ability to accept full responsibility for his life, the good and the bad."
>
> — **Great Igwe**

Taking personal responsibility is crucial for you to be successful. Mediocre people don't ever take personal responsibility for their life. I hope this book propels you to take responsibility for your life. At the end of the day your success is dependent upon you, so rise and take control of your life.

> "One of the greatest challenges in creating a joyful, peaceful and abundant life is taking responsibility for what you do and how you do it. If you can blame someone else, be angry with someone else, point a finger at someone else, you are not taking responsibility for your life."
>
> — **Iyanla Vanzant**

You must take personal responsibility. You cannot change the circumstances, the seasons, or the wind, but you can change yourself. That is something you have charge of. The moment you take responsibility for everything in your life is the moment you can change anything in your life.

Everything you do is based on the choices you make. It's not your parents, your past relationships, your job, the economy, the weather, an argument or your age that is to blame. You and only you are responsible for every decision and choice you make, period. The victim mindset dilutes the human potential. By not accepting personal responsibility for our circumstances, we greatly reduce our power to change them. I'm not telling you it's going to be easy. I'm telling you it's going to be worth it.

> *"The shell must break before the bird can fly."*
>
> — *Alfred Tennyson*

Holding on to grudges and negative feelings from years past will never get you out of the crappy situation you are in. What will get you out of this situation? Planning how you intend to get out and how you intend to achieve success. Writing down your reason! Your purpose! You should say to yourself: no more! No more will I blame others for my situation! The past is gone. I cannot get it back, and I will not complain about it any longer! I will drop it like a hot potato and move on with my life. I will do whatever it takes!

When negative circumstances come, I accept they are not happening to me, rather just happening, as they do to all humans. I will know in that moment I have a chance to accept responsibility or play victim. I will know, only one of those choices will lead to success; the other leads to a life of misery and average living. I choose success; I choose to show character, I choose to be proud of my life! I am in charge here! I take responsibility!

> *"If you could kick the person in the pants responsible*
>
> *For most of your trouble you wouldn't*
>
> *Sit for a month."*
>
> — *Theodore Roosevelt*

You are where you are because of your decisions. If you don't believe this, chances are you are not where you want to be. Take responsibility for your position! You are the only one responsible for your life and the only one capable of making it better. No more playing victim. It's not anyone else's fault you aren't where you want to be. It's yours.

Start Taking Advantage of Your Regrets

One the most challenging aspects of avoiding failure, pain and regret is that it's not until we experience them that we learn how to avoid them. We don't know the stove is hot until we touch it, and we don't know what losing a championship feels like until the final point is scored. The actions that led to these results are ultimately where we went wrong, but in the moments beforehand we have trouble recognizing the signs. Sure, we can listen to a nagging parent who tells us to keep our hands away from hot things and we can hear the words of other people who have experienced similar events. But to truly understand something we need to experience it ourselves.

"I knew that if I failed I wouldn't regret that,

But I knew the one thing I might regret is not trying."

— *Jeff Bezos*

Prepare for Pain and Act Accordingly

Pain can come in several varying forms. It can be the physical pain of an injury or it can be the emotional pain of loss. In both instances, we are often left with one common emotion. Regret.

We can't help but think "what if I just." or "if only I had done..." deep down we know these statements can't do anything to fix the situation, but I believe they serve a greater purpose. The common problem for many people is that in these moments of pain and regret, they tell themselves all the things they wish they would have done differently and they toil over all the ways they will never let this happen again. It's an extremely tense moment, but often we have our greatest revelations in these trying times. Unfortunately, a month or two later, a lot of these ideas and plans fall flat. We forget about how we felt in the moments after defeat. We cannot recall the true depths of our pain.

If you've ever spent an evening binging on fast food and sweets, you probably know the feeling that came afterwards. You feel like you're going to throw up, your mouth is raw from all the sugar and salt, and you feel like you just gained 20 pounds in 2 hours. As you go to sleep that night, you vow to never do that again. Then a month later, you find yourself going out for a late-night fast food run and buying 6 burgers with a side of apple pie and strawberry sundae. Thirty minutes later, regret sinks in once again.

Our brains simply aren't wired to remember everything about an experience. Very often the moment that sticks with us is the peak moment. The highest point of enjoyment. Your brain hardly remembers the sugar crash; it only remembers those initial bites full of bliss. And the further you get away from that experience, the less likely it is for you to be able to recall the pain you experienced. Whether it's a sugar crash or a painful loss, we are very quick to forget the painful lessons we experienced. We let them slip past us and in the end, we are doomed to repeat our past mistakes.

The Three Versions of You

There are always three versions of us:

- The past self
- The present self
- The future self

These versions of ourselves can sometimes seem like different people. We often feel like the decisions made by the past version of ourselves were immature and naïve. And we choose to let the future versions of ourselves deal with the problems when we choose to procrastinate. However, since neither the past nor future versions of ourselves ever actually "exist" in real time, the only person that suffers is the present version.

We lack empathy for ourselves, forgetting what it feels like to be in the shoes of our past self. Failing to remember how painful it was to lose that big match or miss the game winning shot. In the end, we don't learn the lesson. First off, it's difficult to relive an emotion, especially if we never take the time to live with it in the first place.

But with one simple practice, it's possible to properly address this issue. The next time you experience a painful moment, record how you were feeling afterwards. The regrets you had, the wishes you were making and the promises you made to yourself. Ask yourself the following questions:

- What are you feeling right now?
- Why are you disturbed by this feeling?
- How could you have handled the situation better?
- What will you do to never let this happen again?

Once you've done that, pull out your phone and politely tell Siri or Google Assistant to set a reminder one month from now. A month later when that reminder chimes in, go back and review what you wrote down. Reflect and figure out if you are still on track. If you aren't, refer to the answer you gave to the question, "what will you do to never let this happen again?"

> "The only permanent solution to your problems is to go inside and let go of the part of you that seems to have so many problems with reality. Once you do that, you'll be clear enough to deal with what's left."
>
> — *Michael Singer*

In a world with so many varying opinions, values, beliefs, and lifestyles, many of us are quick to judge the actions of others. But before we can do that, we need to be able to properly judge ourselves. We must take the time to listen to our inner dialogue and understand where it's coming from. Our brains are wired to avoid things that cause us pain. We instinctively want to protect ourselves. We should do a better job of helping this voice be heard on a regular basis.

By implementing a practice like the one mentioned above, we give ourselves a fighting chance and we allow that inner voice to be heard more clearly. In this present moment, listen to the past version of yourself so that the future version of yourself can live the life you really want to live without any regret.

When you take full responsibility for your life, you are no longer a player in life's team, taking whatever comes your way; you become the captain, the coach, the director of your life's experience and you really can design it how you like.

Chapter Eight

GIVE UP ON GIVING UP

This is your only life. You have only one shot at it. Whether you fail or succeed, it all depends on you; not on God, your parents, the government, or your spouse. No, it's up to you to make it count. The battle is yours to fight alone, and the victory will also be yours to celebrate. Don't give in, don't throw in the towel now. It's hard to take the next step, it's difficult to accept another punch from life, but if you persist to the end it will all be worth it.

Stop blaming the circumstances of your birth. Stop blaming your dad who left your mum to take care of you all by herself. Stop blaming your spouse for not doing this or that for you. Stop blaming the government for the misfortunes in your life. Stop blaming God. Like it or not, inherent in every person on earth, is an imbedded ability to succeed despite your predicament. In the next chapter I will share with you many great and successful people with different stories and circumstances of birth who have defied the limitations placed on them from birth and have risen to become the agents of change and success we celebrate today; those who rose from nothing, from "nobodies" to men and women of great recognition; and lastly those who have fought several challenges in life from finance, career, relationship and purpose to become living testimonies to the validity of the fact that persistence pays.

> *"It always seems impossible*
>
> *Until it's done."*
>
> *— Nelson Mandela*

An important lesson that I learned in my past is to never ever give up: always persevere. If you fall, then get back up and try again. It doesn't matter if it is the first time, or the millionth time, you must always get back up again. Regardless of what challenges you are facing, you must keep pushing forward. Life isn't going to slow down for you, so you must work to keep up. Each time you get up, that is more character, more strength you have developed. It is always important to set goals for yourself. Never stop reaching for the stars. Sometimes tomorrow is about learning from yesterday.

There are so many famous people from whom we can learn to never ever give up. One such big name is Oprah Winfrey. She's famous not only for being the iconic face on the TV, but also for never giving up and sticking to her dreams. She had a rough childhood and faced many setbacks in her career, which included her being fired for being "unfit for Television news".

> *"In the confrontation between the stream and the rock,*
>
> *The stream always wins*
>
> *Not through strength but by perseverance."*
>
> *— H. Jackson Brown*

"Never give up" is one of the most used phrases given as advice. Honestly, it's easier said than done, because the one in that "about-to-give-up" position knows how difficult it is. For someone who's caught in a rough phase, it's easy to give up but is it really what you want? That one dream you've been dreaming all your life, would you just give it up because of the innumerable problems you're facing? Simply reading success stories won't help, acting upon it will. Just remember, these obstacles are temporary and will soon disappear from your way!

Remember those convincing dialogues from the movies, those sarcastic funny quotes which make you think about altering your attitude towards life. Don't just think, start acting upon them. Take baby steps, stay determined all the way, and then you're free to fulfill all that you ever wanted.

Sometimes persevering means that you need to start over. If you are feeling depressed, you might need to make an important change in your life. For example, if you are unhappy in your career, you might need to consider a new job or business. If you are unsatisfied with your partner, you may need to make changes in your relationship, or find somebody new. If you are feeling down, it means that you have flat lined. You need to make the changes that are necessary to push your life in a positive direction.

> *"Many of life's failures are people who*
>
> *Did not realize how close they were*
>
> *To success when they gave up."*
>
> *— Thomas Edison*

Another important fact to consider is that you don't have to succeed at everything you do. Sometimes it just matters that you showed up to try. If you are unhappy with your performance, you can always try again tomorrow. People talk themselves out of trying because they are afraid of making a mistake. You can always make a mistake, and that is not an excuse to not even try or a reason to back out.

Some of the most famous people and companies started from humble beginnings. In their first year of business, Coca-Cola only sold 400 bottles of Coke. Michael Jordan was cut from his high school basketball team. Dr. Seuss' first children's book, *And to Think That I Saw It on Mulberry Street*, was rejected by 27 publishers. Vanguard Press, the 28th publisher, sold 6 million copies of the book. The book, *Chicken Soup for the Soul* was turned down by 33 publishers before Health Communications, Inc. agreed to publish it. Since then, over 7 million copies of *Chicken Soup for the Soul*, *A 2nd Helping of Chicken Soup for the Soul* and *The Chicken Soup for the Soul Cookbook* have been sold worldwide, with the books translated into 20 languages.

If Michael Jordan, Dr. Seuss, Coca-Cola, and the authors of *Chicken Soup for the Soul* had given up, then they wouldn't be the household names that they are today. These inspirational stories serve as living proof that if at first you don't succeed, you must try and try again.

> *"Most of the important things in the world have been accomplished by people who have kept on trying when there seemed to be no hope at all."*
>
> — *Dale Carnegie*

You must also appreciate the people who appreciate you. If somebody isn't doing the right thing by you, then ask them to either change their ways or move on. You deserve nothing less than the best, and it is your responsibility to produce your best work for others. This is not limited to physical work, but also includes spiritual work. There is never a day when you can't create or accomplish a new goal. Let life be a learning experience. Don't let this year be another year of good intentions with unaccomplished goals. If you want to accomplish something, then you need to do something about it!

To never ever give up doesn't always mean you should keep at a useless cause. It means never ever give up on that great life you deserve. You might have to change your approach – the "how" you will get there – but just never ever give up on your dream life. There is always a way if you are willing to find a way!

Have the Courage to Face Your Fears and Live Your Dreams

It is incredibly enlightening to fully appreciate and recognize that it is possible to achieve anything that you set your mind to. Once you understand that you possess the capability of achieving whatever it is that you set out to do in life, you will undoubtedly feel more excited about the present time, and more motivated about attaining your goals in the future.

> *"It does not matter how slowly you go*
>
> *As long as you do not stop."*
>
> *— Confucius*

So, how can you learn to trust that everything is going to work out for you in life, and how can you begin to see all possibilities in life as being limitless? It's certainly not easy to remain focused or excited to keep moving forward when times are uncertain or difficult. I believe that the key, my reader friends, has to do with being courageous, believing in yourself and being true to who you are.

Being courageous and brave is everything. It is vital to have faith in yourself, to be true to yourself and to have the courage to do what it takes to achieve your goal. This consists of having the courage to be completely honest with whom you are and being strong enough to face your fears, anxieties and struggles head-on.

> "We don't choose the circumstances surrounding our birth,
>
> But we sure have the power to choose
>
> How our life turns out to be."
>
> — *Bishop Harry Jackson Jr*

George Bernard Shaw once wrote, "People are always blaming circumstances for what they are. I don't believe in circumstances. The people who get ahead in this world are the people who get up and look for the circumstances they want, and if they can't find them, make them."

Pursuing your passions and being yourself requires a tremendous amount of inner strength, and it's important to constantly recognize and appreciate the confidence that it takes to follow your heart and your dreams! Often, following your passion and doing what you feel is right for your life will involve going out on your own, being independent, and standing strong in your choices. Even when others may disagree with your decisions, if you feel that what you're doing is right for your life, then it is important to stand firm in what you have chosen to do and who you have chosen to be.

> "Our greatest weakness lies in giving up. The most certain way to succeed is always to try just one more time."
>
> — *Thomas Edison*

When you make a commitment to be true to yourself and to your dreams, the possibilities for your life truly are endless. The first step in becoming a more courageous individual, is to take an honest look at who you are today and think about the person you'd like to become tomorrow.

Take some time to think about what it is that you believe will bring even more happiness to your life and tell yourself that it is possible to achieve anything! Don't doubt yourself. The key is being courageous and being brave enough to try. Earl Nightingale said, *"We become what we think about."* Think about what is possible for you and who you can become and get out there to make all your dreams your reality.

Do not hold yourself back, my friend. You're the only one who can stop yourself from reaching your highest potential, and it's crucial that you don't get in your own way. We are all dealing with certain struggles, but you are a lot stronger than you might even realize. It is time to let go of any doubt and begin to move forward through any struggles that you might be facing. You're strong enough to conquer any challenge if you're not afraid to try.

"When you get into a tight place and everything goes against you, till it seems as though you could not hang on a minute longer, never give up then, for that is just the place and time that the tide will turn."

— Harriet Beecher Stowe

You have much to offer this world. Let go of any fears or worries and decide to make this year the one that will lead you on a path to your highest potential. The reality is that you have nothing to lose, except for the negative thoughts that chain you down! Henry David Thoreau said, "Go confidently in the direction of your dreams. Live the life that you've imagined." Decide to be courageous and to live truthfully. By doing so, you will begin to break free from fear and set yourself up to reach your full potential.

> "Courage does not always roar. Sometimes courage is the quiet voice at the end of the day saying, 'I will try again tomorrow.'"
>
> — *Mary Anne Radmacher*

Never Settle for Less

The only limitations are those you set up in your own mind. There is no such thing as impossible. If you can believe it, then you can achieve it. There is no such thing as limitations. The only thing holding you back is yourself. Your own views of what is, and, what is not possible. It's easy to get deflated when others don't believe in you. Especially those that might be close to you. There are always going to be those that say it can't be done.

> "Life is like riding a bicycle.
>
> To keep your balance,
>
> You must keep moving."
>
> — *Albert Einstein*

Their thoughts and feelings will beat you down! They will knock you down to the ground. But I'll tell you what you are going to do. You will get back on your feet! Because you know there is more inside you than they will ever know. You know your greatness! They know nothing. They don't know your courage. You know! They don't know the fight in you.

They don't know the sacrifices you are willing to make! You know! They do not know that you will stop at nothing to achieve your goals. How hard you will work to reach that dream you have. They don't know you have the heart of a lion, the courage of a thousand men, and the strength of this universe at your back.

No one has the right to tell you otherwise. No one knows your true capability. Prove them wrong! Live your dreams! Be fearless. You did not wake up this morning to be mediocre! Push harder. One day will be your day. Never let it go, never settle, never! Never! Never! Get it done! There are no more excuses. Excuses don't live here anymore. Excuses aren't invited to this party. Excuses are a virus. Get them out of your life.

> "Success seems to be largely a matter of
>
> Hanging on after others have let go."
>
> — *William Feather*

What Do You Want to Be?

Are you going to show some courage to take yourself to another level? The level you know you deserve? To join the 1%, you have to be doing things the other 99% aren't willing to do. The last set, the last blood, the last mile — that's where life separates the greats from the average and small. That's where the 1% rise to the top.

> "Sometimes you have to be unconventional and controversial to actually bring the desired changed you want to see in life."
>
> — *Great Igwe*

You see, to have the things that others don't you need to be willing to do the things that others won't. Are you willing? Are you willing to give one more try? Are you willing to throw in one more punch? Are you willing to go the extra mile to grab your dreams? To reach your goal?!

> *"Don't give up. There are too many nay-sayers*
> *Out there who will try to discourage you. Don't listen to them.*
> *The only one who can make you give up is yourself."*
>
> **— Sidney Sheldon**

Sacrifice now. Enjoy later. Push hard now, relax later. If you believe it's possible you can achieve the impossible. Believe in yourself! You can do it! No limits! No boundaries! No doubts! The world is your playground and you only get one shot. Make it count. There is nothing more satisfying than making it on your own terms. Make it happen. Unleash the lion inside of you!

> *"Greatness is not this wonderful, esoteric, elusive, god-like feature that only the special among us will ever taste you know, it's something that truly exists in all of us. It's very simple: this is what I believe and I'm willing to die for it. Period. It's that simple."*
>
> **— Will Smith**

Pushing past difficulties and surmounting adversities, especially in the face of very trying times, is a monumental undertaking. To add to that, when you have the regular stresses of everyday life that include things like your finances, children, spouses or significant others, and the fact that you must deal with life's random crises, it can be too much to handle.

> "A diamond is a chunk of coal that did
>
> Well under pressure."
>
> — *Henry Kissinger*

However, getting through the tough times in life can be just a little bit easier when you can rely on certain methods. When you can fall back on strategies that have worked throughout the ages, the tough times might not seem so tough. That's not to say that life's difficulties will immediately disappear. No, they won't. You'll simply realize the importance of the beauty, simplicity and miracle of life.

While this might sound utopian in nature, it isn't. Life is beautiful. Life is a gift. It's been given to us by our Creator.

Look, I've had my fair share of tough times in life. I've suffered through the pain and torment of failure. I cannot even begin to describe the heartache that I have been through. So, I know how it feels. I know that life isn't all sunshine and rainbows. But I do know that life is what you make of it. As Forest Gump once said, "Mama always said life was like a box of chocolates. You never know what you're going to get."

> "You have within you right now,
>
> Everything you need to deal with whatever
>
> The world can throw at you."
>
> — *Brian Tracy*

Whatever we're going through today, someone else has gone through. Over the course of the centuries and millenniums, human beings have had to suffer through tough times. While only a short span of that time is available in recorded history, one can only imagine what our ancestors went through, things that will likely never see the light of day.

So regardless of how much difficulty you're facing, or how much strife you're in now, tough times don't last. While I don't profess to have all the answers, I do know a thing or two about disappointment and failure and overcoming difficult circumstances in life.

You Must Be Odd to Be Different

It doesn't matter what is or isn't possible for others. It doesn't matter how small the percentages are for success. The only thing that matters is what you believe is possible for you. What do you believe? If you are going to be a statistic: be in the 1%, the minority that do believe. The minority that do achieve despite their setbacks and limitations.

They say you are the average of the 5 people you spend the most time with. I say, someone must be setting the standard. Statistics will tell you it's impossible to make it. Only a fraction succeeds in life. Huge failure rate! Statistics will say only a very small percentage make it in business. A smaller percentage have their ideal body, even less their ideal income, less again live a life they are happy with.

But it doesn't matter what statistics say. What do you say? Does your mindset tell you if 99% fail, the odds are against you? Or does your mindset see opportunity? Does your mindset see the remaining 1% that makes up the 100? Are you the 1%? Does your mindset know that you have something uniquely special inside of you and you can have, be and do whatever you want in life?

The greats don't care about statistics, they only care for one thing. One thing that's much bigger than statistics: the successful know anything is possible. They understand there are no limits except those you create in your own mind. The greats know their desire to succeed is much greater than fear of statistics. Much greater than fear of failure. Successful human beings know with absolute certainty that their heart, passion, determination, desire and relentlessness will always see them reach the top in the end.

They know there may be failures and setbacks along the way, but their desire to reach their goals will always be greater than any setback. They don't quit after setbacks or failures! They work harder. They learn lessons. They grow their character during the hard times. Statistics don't mean anything to those with belief!

> *"The secret of change is to focus all of your energy,*
>
> *Not on fighting the old, but on building the new."*
>
> *— Dan Millman*

Don't be a statistic, find your purpose. Do whatever it takes to succeed, regardless of setbacks, regardless of what the statistics tell you or what others think of you. The only thing that matters is your opinion of yourself. Your belief in yourself. The truth is, it doesn't matter what the stats say. It doesn't matter if the odds are against you. It doesn't matter if no one else believes in you. What matters is you believing in yourself, knowing in your own heart that you will make it in the end; that you will scale through, triumph, and bounce back.

Don't settle for a mediocre life just because the stats show most take the easy road. They can say what they like! Tell you it's "impossible". Tell you it's never been done. Show them it is possible when the job is done!

Rise up with boldness and confront your battle. You can come out of this; you can still live your dreams. You can still bounce back. Don't let his/her death or departure tear you apart. You did your best, you gave your best, you stayed faithful, but life has taken it course. Now you must move on. You must live your own life. A new page starts from you now.

New Beginnings

Everybody loves to see miraculous transformations. Whether it's a sports team that goes from worst to first in a single season, a life-saving surgery for a child, a person that loses hundreds of pounds, or even the amazing home makeover on TV that takes a home in much need of TLC, and literally transforms it into a beautiful haven. We all love the outcome of miraculous transformations.

Anytime we want to have a change though, especially one that will make our lives better, it requires us to believe that it can happen. We must make a choice to have hope. Most of us have found ourselves in a place where we were on the edge of losing something very precious, or seemingly everything. Whether you've lost your job, your mortgage is in risk of foreclosure, your relationships are struggling, or you or a loved one needs healing, I want to encourage you to never give up!

It all begins with a choice; the choice to never give up. God always completes in us what he has started; His good work and good plan.

"Being confident of this, that he who began a good work in you will carry it on to completion until the day of Christ Jesus."

— Philippians 1:6 (NIV)

I love the story of a man named Ira Yates. His story is the perfect example of what happens when you never give up. By the time he was 12, both of his parents had died. He and his brothers had no choice but to take care of themselves. So, they got jobs working at a ranch. Through hard work and refusing to give up, Ira eventually got married and saved enough to buy a small ranch of his own. He kept dreaming, staying focused and making good decisions.

He bought a small grocery store, which turned into a big success. But he didn't stop there either. He then sold the store to purchase a large 20,000-acre ranch in west Texas.

Not long after this big move, the great depression hit with full force and Ira fell behind on his payments. The bank threatened to foreclose and take away everything he'd worked so hard for through the years. At the last moment, just days before Ira lost everything; massive reservoirs of oil were discovered on his ranch! Instead of losing everything, Ira received more than enough resources to bless his entire family and many more throughout his area. He provided jobs for people in need, built schools, children's homes, Boy Scout camps, Salvation Army centers and developed a town that still exists today. I love this story because his life was suddenly transformed.

"Just remember: to be great you have to be willing to be

Mocked, hated, and misunderstood. Stay strong."

*— **Rumah Sehat***

Now I'm not saying that you're going to find oil on your property or instantly become a millionaire! But what I am saying is that no matter how dark things look, God can turn things around in a single moment.

We all just enjoyed the changing of seasons, from winter to spring. Spring symbolizes new birth, a fresh start. No matter how cold and harsh your winter might have seemed, or even been, I want to encourage you to see your new fresh start in god. It all starts with your mind and attitude. Even if you don't physically see this change right now, God can transform your heart and thinking, giving you peace that the world can't give you. It's a sustaining peace. It's hope. Hope carries you through as you wait for your completing moment.

"Anyone can give up, it's the easiest thing in the world to do. But to hold it together when everyone else would understand if you fell apart, that's true strength."

— Bishop Harry Jackson

Ephesians 1:19–20 (NLT) says: *"I pray that you will understand the incredible greatness of God's power for us who believe him. This is the same mighty power that raised Christ from the dead."* Think about it! The Bible says that God gives the same power that raised Jesus from the dead to those who believe Him. He triumphed over every force of darkness, disease and destruction. And He's promised to give this same victory to everyone who puts their trust in Him! God's incredible power is available for you, but you must do your part: believe in Him and by faith, receive what He is offering and persevere in your hope!

When you face challenges and tough times, do you focus on the negative and begin to complain about how unfairly you are being treated? When you give in to those thoughts, you stop the transformation process. When you are filled with doubt and unbelief, God's miracle for you is put on hold. And it stays on hold until you begin to walk again in obedience and put your complete trust in Him.

When you stay positive, full of hope, and do not give up on God, He can take any situation in your life, any circumstance, regardless of the economy or what the world might say, and turn things around in a single moment for your benefit. Your life can change in a moment just like Ira's and just like the lives of the disciples who went from being alone and afraid to boldly proclaiming the message of Christ to every nation, making an impact on the entire world!

> *"Next to trying and winning,*
>
> *The best thing is trying and failing."*
>
> — *Lucy Maud Montgomery*

No matter what you are facing today, I want to encourage you, when you decide to not give up and put your whole trust in Christ, you pave the way for greater things to happen for you, in you and through you! His word promises us in Philippians 4:19 (AMP): *"and my God will liberally supply (fill to the full) your every need according to his riches in glory in Christ Jesus"*. God promises us that He can meet every need. Remember, no matter what challenges you're facing, God will make all things new in your life! But it's up to you and your choice! Keep choosing to stay in hope, believing for God to make things new, in His time. Remember, if we don't give up, in due time we will be richly rewarded!

There are goals that we all want to accomplish and situations we're believing will turn around. But so often when it's taking a long time, the negative thoughts come that say, "it's never going to change." "You're never going to get well." "You're never going to get out of debt." "That child is never going to straighten up." If we're not careful, we'll get discouraged and end up just settling where we are.

Many times, we miss out on God's best because we gave up too soon. Just another few days of believing, another few weeks of doing the right thing, or another few months of staying in faith, and we would see that promise come to pass.

> *"A winner is just a loser*
>
> *Who tried one more time?"*
>
> *— George M. Moore Jr.*

Hebrews 10:35 tells us that if we will stay in faith, if we will keep believing, keep hoping, keep doing the right thing, God promises there will be a reward. One translation says, "Don't get discouraged. Payday is coming." When you're tempted to feel down and things are not going your way, you need to keep telling yourself, "This may be hard. It may be taking a long time, but I know God is a faithful God, and I'm going to believe, knowing that my payday is on its way!"

It time to say goodbye to the past and embrace the future. Now is the time to let loose that lion in you. That super hero in you. Don't allow this circumstance to tear you apart because you are stronger and more capable than you think, if you must win, then you must be ready to stand up and say enough is enough. You have to say, this time I take charge, I take control. You are too strong to be tossed around; you are too capable to be easily defeated. This is the test that will write your story on the sands of memory.

Chapter Nine

ANYTHING IS POSSIBLE IF YOU BELIEVE

When we think about what we are capable of, we never think big enough. We look at others and we believe that somehow, they have something we don't and that perhaps they were always destined for more. We tell ourselves that we don't have it in us to live that way and to take the action that they do. We worry that we're not brave enough to make the decisions needed to really live from a place of truth. Or worse, we fear we have nothing of value to offer! These are all stories to keep us small and playing safe.

We have all these fears bubbling away inside us; the fear of failing, being seen, being rejected, being judged or even criticized for what we believe in. Instead of facing them head on, we choose to run and hide and in doing so we deprive the world of our gifts! Maybe you're someone who fears success itself… because who would you then have to be? What would have to change in your life? What would you no longer tolerate? Who would you lovingly release and let go of?

Even when change is for the best it's still scary! No one enjoys difficult conversations or potentially hurting someone's feelings, and this can stop many people from fulfilling their potential! But, do you really want to dim your light for the sake of another? Is their happiness more important than your own?

It's time to stop limiting yourself. You are much stronger than you could imagined. Whatever is thrown at you, I know you'll deal with it… plus, you always have God in your corner for support! If you can see and feel the dream in your mind, then it is possible. Know that you have so much to give and share and the world is waiting for you and only you. We are all special and unique expressions of the divine and someone needs your talents and skills, with your unique voice and story! No one else will do. It's time to step up, believe in yourself, and dream big!

Life is not predetermined; it's crafted daily. Remember, the only thing stopping you from achieving the dream is yourself. Do you really want to waste a few more years blaming things outside yourself, only to have to face the cold hard reality that it was you all along? If you want this year to be your year, then you need to commit to yourself and your dreams now. Stop putting things off until you feel readier, or the time is perfect. I guarantee there will never be a right time, because your ego will always find something else to focus on to keep you safe.

"If I have the belief that I can do it,

I shall surely acquire the capacity to do it

Even if I may not have it at the beginning."

— Mahatma Ghandi

It doesn't matter what anyone says you can or can't do. It doesn't matter what opinions others have for your life, and what they consider possible. If you believe in yourself, then anything is possible! Why is it we don't believe in ourselves? That as soon as things get tough in our lives we start doubting ourselves? We start thinking that we may not make it, stressing, worrying, imagining things that may go wrong in the future.

We need to understand, the human mind is the most powerful tool we own, but it can also be the most destructive and we need to learn how to take control of the direction of our mind and our emotions. Your mind is going to provide you your greatest challenges in life, because it is very powerful so, if you can conquer your mind, you can pretty much conquer anything else around you, literally.

When writing the story of your life make sure you hold the pen. Make sure you not only hold the pen, but you write the script from your heart. Be brave when writing your script, it's your story and there are no limits to what you can have, what you can do or what you can be. You must prove to yourself that you want it bad enough. It's got to hurt you not to get it.

And that's when you're going to learn to conquer your mind. Your mind will no longer be able to say no, because your inner heart and mind are aligned, and now nothing can stop you! It's easy to be all positive and consistent when everything is going your way. But that's not life, that's not realistic! Are you going to be one of the very few to stand up when things are tough, when everything is going against you? Will you be able to believe in what's right, and what brings results to your life?

That's when your character will shine! That's when your story will be born! Your story is valuable! Your story of success! And you can't build a story if you stop now, if you give up. The world is full of people who gave up. The world needs hope. We all do. The world needs you to stand up to fight through your challenging moments, to shine through the dark times, to love through the hate, and to be the difference in an indifferent world. To believe in yourself.

Most people are bloated with ordinary thoughts and mindsets. They're so full of average that they have no more appetite, but you must have an appetite for extraordinary beyond what people are doing. Think beyond them. There will always be doubters, people below you, and people trying to put you down so they can feel higher, but you've got to stay true to yourself. Believe in your mind. Then one day you will have your moment. Because anything is possible if you just believe!

What is Impossible? Nothing.

I have seen people come from nothing and later in life, they became great and celebrated. I see people start off with nothing in their pockets, but before they died, they built an empire of wealth. It's because they could see exactly what they wanted, a long time ago. If you can think it inside your brain, it can come to life. If someone else has achieved it before, you can too. And I guarantee you, whatever you seek, there will be a reference of someone achieving it, somewhere on this great planet.

Find the story, model them, and then better them. It matters not the color of your skin. It matters not where you were born. It matters not the limits of your friends and family. The only thing that matters is you and what you believe is possible. Make sure the answer is anything! Anything is possible. But only if that is what you believe. See, if you are the type that says no, anything isn't possible, that will also be your reality. If you believe there are limits to what you can achieve based on the excuses you put down, like your limited opportunity, like where you live, like lack of funds — well, those limits become your reality because you won't even attempt something outside of your limited mindset.

The one that believes anything is possible will try anything. Will attempt greatness. Will risk everything to be anything but average. And even if they miss the target, they will be far ahead of the one that never tries. When you believe in yourself anything is possible. So many have risen from nothing to something. From hopeless to greatness. From no resources, they built a legacy. If they can do it, you can too. But only if you believe. Now it's one thing to believe anything is possible, but something else entirely to achieve something incredible.

So, get out there and plan. When you suffer setbacks and failures, keep going and learn the lessons. Everyone going after something great will experience setbacks. You must keep going. Make the plan better, stronger. Anything is possible. Anything is possible! Anything is possible! Change that ugly picture that you see in your head. How dare you tell yourself that you don't have what it takes, when you were born with a gift?

"It's a lie to think you're not good enough.

It's a lie to think you're not worth anything."

— Nick Vujicic

You were born with a purpose. You were born with opportunity. To grow every day, to become better every day. Cherish the small things that are big in your heart and watch greatness be created. Feed your dreams. If you can suffer through setbacks, through pain, rise with resilience once again, and again, and again, one day this world will tap you on the shoulder and say, "This is your time to shine."

You can have and do anything you want, if you believe.

Decide that you are ready, and this is your time. Decide that you are going to impact the world with your unique gifts and you will change lives. Decide that you are ready to share your story and truth and know that the world will hear and embrace it! Listen to those quiet whispers because your soul is calling you.

This is not your end. You can come out of this, and you can bounce back again stronger and better. It's time for you to start believing in yourself and what is possible for your life.

There once was a girl who ran very slow,

Her true potential she did not know.

In every race she always placed last,

Losing all hope as she got passed.

Her coach encouraged her to just do her best,

Although it hurt her that she couldn't run with the rest.

She went to practice day after day,

Praying to God "Just let me run away."

She wanted to quit, she hated the pain.

She didn't know what she had to gain.

One day while she sat at home all alone,

She heard a ring and answered the phone.

"Hello?" she asked in a sad voice.

The caller told her she had but one choice;

"You can cry in pity, you can hide in shame

Or do what you must to get back in the game."

"Excuse me...but," she began to say.

"No excuses," he replied, "Now be on your way."

She didn't know how, she didn't know why.

She just knew that she must try.

Later that week she ran in a race,

Starting off faster at a quicker pace.

She knew that no one believed she could win;

She was all on her own using strength from within.

As the miles went on, she felt really strong,

Chasing her goal as she went along.

Suddenly the finish line was in her sight,

She knew she could hang on for a finishing fight.

She began to sprint and open her stride.

The crowd cheered on and she filled with pride.

At the finish she was leaning over the line,

Winning as first with a record time.

She looked at her coach, who smiled and said,

"I knew you could do it! It was all in your head!"

A reporter walked up and asked of her name,

"How did you do it? Do you like the fame?"

Questions were asked all and about,

But there was only thing she wanted to shout:

"Anything is possible when you believe

You can attain whatever you set out to achieve."

With that comment she turned with a smile, for

"One man's marathon... is another's mile."

— **Lisa N. Redavid**

Fear kills dreams. Fear kills hope. Fear can age you. It can hold you back from doing something that you know within yourself that you can do, paralyzing you. Every day you say "no" to your dreams, you might be pushing your dreams back a whole six months, a whole year! That one single day, that one day you didn't get up could have pushed your stuff back, I don't know how long. Don't allow your emotions to control you. We are emotional, but begin to discipline your emotions. If you don't discipline and contain your emotions, they will use you. You want it and you're going to go all out to have it. It's not going to be easy. When you want to change, it's not easy. If it were in fact easy, everybody would do it. But if you're serious, you will go all out.

> "You must find the place inside yourself where
>
> Nothing is impossible."
>
> — Deepak Chopra

I'm in control here. I'm not going to let this get me down, I'm not going to let this destroy me. I'm coming back. And I'll be stronger and better because of it. You've got to make a declaration. That this is what you stand for. You're standing up for your dreams, you're standing up for peace of mind, and you're standing up for health. Take full responsibility for your life. Accept where you are and the responsibility that you're going to take yourself where you want to go. You can decide that you're going to live each day as if it were your last. Live your life with passion. With some drive.

> "If you believe you can, you probably can.
>
> If you believe you won't, you most assuredly won't.
>
> Belief is the ignition switch that gets you off the launching pad."
>
> — Denis Waitley

Decide that you're going to push yourself. The last chapter to your life has not been written yet, and it doesn't matter what happened yesterday. It doesn't matter what happened to you. What matters is what you're going to do about it.

> *"Many of the things that seem impossible*
>
> *Now will become realities of tomorrow."*
>
> — **Walt Disney**

Are You Going to be a Lion or a Sheep?

It's time to unleash the fighter in you. The easiest thing to do is to give up. The hardest thing is to keep going when the chips are down. To keep pushing when things are hard. Oh yeah, it's easy to put on the happy face when everything is going well. What about when you are facing pain, defeat, failure? What have you got inside? Have you got the strength to carry on? Do you have the will to fight back?

Are you going to be a lion or a sheep? The king of the jungle or another insignificant number in the herd? A leader or a follower? A respected boss or slave to a boss? You see, a sheep is someone who expects the things he wants to be given to him. A lion is someone who goes out and hunts for the things he wants. You are the captain of your fate. The master of your soul. The boss of your dreams. The king of your goals. You can have, be, and do anything! You just got to believe. One day will be your day, then you will achieve! The truth is you know within your heart you have what it takes. Many have come before you with less and achieved more. Many have reached the peak of success. And now, now it's your turn!

> *"The difference between the impossible*
>
> *And the possible lies in a person's determination."*
>
> — *Nelson Mandela*

Chapter Ten

IF THEY CAN DO IT, YOU CAN

We all need motivation in life. We all need some super heroes to learn from, people that we can see, and get inspired. And the world is full of many of such great people with different stories and unique journeys through life's seas and storms. Many times, when the storms of life hit us, we tend to think the worst. We condition our minds to believe that we are alone in this world or that our situation is the worst of its kind. This mindset is not only false but dilapidating.

> *"Failure is unimportant.*
> *It takes courage to make a fool of yourself."*
>
> — **Charlie Chaplin**

Throughout history, there have been thousands of famous failures. Even before recorded history, people were battling with the push-and-pull created by this burning desire to succeed. This goes beyond mere survival. Survival is built into our DNA. It's part of the very fabric that makes us who we are.

However, human beings weren't just made to survive; we were made to thrive. We've been thriving since the earliest days of our species some 200,000 years ago. With the beautiful invention of language, we've been able to expand our knowledge, enhance our technology and vastly improve our quality of life. Still, while we're suffering through the disheartening and gut-wrenching pains of failure, we're often not thinking about thriving, we're solely focused on surviving. When we fail, it makes us question everything, right down to the very heart of who we are and why we've been put here on this earth. But failure, as much as it hurts, is also a necessary part of life. It's the pathway to our goals.

In fact, the most successful and famous people in the world have endured the most failures in life. They've failed repeatedly. But they've also gotten back up. They didn't throw in that proverbial towel. They didn't call it quits or head for the ropes. They got up and kept going. And that's just what it takes to succeed.

Today, if you've suffered through failures in the past, or you're going through the torrent of a failure right now, know this: failure will make you better. Failure will improve your life. It will allow you to reach new understandings and epiphanies on life, love, business and the people all around you. Still, it's not enough to talk about failure in that aspect. It's not enough to talk about the theoretical power that failure has. It's far more beneficial to look at some of the most famous people in time who've failed. It's far easier to rely on their experiences and witness what they had to suffer through, than it is to just reflect on failure itself.

Remember, you're never too old to try again. It's never too late to take another shot. Some famous failures were in their 60's when they gave it another go such as Colonel Harland Sanders, the founder of KFC, who was 65 years old when he set out with nothing more than a $105 social security check in his pocket and a recipe for his now-famous fried chicken.

You get the idea? Never give up on your hopes and your dreams. Never let someone else tell you that you're not good enough, smart enough or talented enough to achieve greatness in whatever capacity you're seeking. You can do anything you put your mind to.

The truth is that no matter what circumstance of life you find yourself in, there are people out there who are experiencing same, or similar. The good news is a few decided not to allow their storms drown them. They decided they were never going to give up or settle for an average existence simply because of the limitations facing them. These people are humans like you and I; they have one head and two eyes. Some of them even went through tougher and more painful events in their lives and today the story is different. You read about them in books, you see them on TV, you admire them, and I'm certain you ask yourself sometimes, what is their secret?

I will share their secrets with you, but let me first of share with you the stories of some of these heroes of change; how they walked through the dark tunnels of life, enduring the pains, neglect, discrimination, abuse, rejection, denials, betrayals, and even death to meet light finally. Before you admire the success, first study the story, because for every glory there is a hidden scar of the battle that has been fought secretly.

I call these people my everyday heroes, because they inspire me each day to thrive and be the best I can be. Remember, the greatest hero is one who has conquered himself, his fear and his battles. Their stories inspire me and give me courage to press on despite the limitations and setbacks.

HERO NUMBER 1: ***SYLVESTER STALLONE:***

Sylvester Stallone has been a household name for decades after the monster success of the *Rocky* franchise that began in the 1970s. Not only did he star in these movies as Rocky, he also directed, produced, and wrote most of the films. *Rocky* was his first big hit that made him a certified movie star, and today, at age 73, he is still acting, writing, and directing feature films. While he makes success look easy, that was not always the case. Here is the unbelievable inspiring story of Sylvester Stallone; a true rag to riches story. Like many actors, Stallone struggled at the beginning of his Hollywood career. But his struggles were more than most. He was so broke that he became homeless, sold his wife's jewelry, and even sold his dog for $25 as he had no money to feed him anymore. He said that was the lowest moment of his entire life and walked away crying.

A few weeks after the tragic event he watched a Mohammed Ali boxing match that inspired him to write *Rocky*. He was so inspired that he wrote the entire script in less than a day! Studios loved the script but didn't love Sylvester Stallone's one request to be the main lead in the movie.

> *"Every time I've failed,*
>
> *People had me out of the count,*
>
> *But I always come back in."*
>
> — ***Sylvester Stallone***

He was offered over $300,000 for the script but still said no — despite being dead broke! He knew that this movie was his ticket to success. After a while, a studio agreed to let him star and only gave him $35,000 for the script. Several things happened.

First, he went back to the place where he sold his dog, waited around long enough, and was able to buy him back. For $3,000! But it wasn't a problem as *Rocky* went on to make history. With a small budget of one million dollars, it went on to gross 225 million dollars, be nominated for several Oscars, and yield six sequels. The best part of this inspirational story is that you can learn two main principles to help you succeed:

Always Believe in Yourself

If Sylvester Stallone had sold his script for $350,000 without acting in the film, he probably wouldn't be the worldwide movie star he is today. He believed in himself with absolute conviction and didn't let money deter him, despite being broke. Don't take the short-term gain if it sacrifices your long-term potential.

Life Can Be Hard Before it's Easy

Sylvester Stallone went from being dead broke and sleeping in a bus station, to being worth 400 million dollars today! If he had given up on his dream of being an actor, it's almost guaranteed he would never have made that kind of money. Don't give up on your dreams just because things are tough right now. When it's bad and you feel scared, tired and think about quitting, keep moving forward!

HERO NUMBER 2: ***JACK MA***

Jack Ma is the founder of the e-commerce giant Alibaba and is a stakeholder at Alipay, its sister company which is an e-payment portal. He is now officially the richest man in China with an estimated net worth of $25 billion, on the back of the recent world record $150 billion filing of his company. Although Alibaba and Jack Ma are not household names outside of China, you must know that Alibaba is worth more than Facebook, and processes goods more than eBay and Amazon combined!

This might be beginning to seem like the story of an arrogant and rich billionaire who hasn't seen the dark. But don't be misled by the numbers that you see above, they can fool anyone. As simple as it may sound, Jack Ma has had it hard in his life to get to where he is today. A true rags-to-riches story and one which will inspire you even on your darkest days.

Ma Yun a.k.a. Jack Ma is one of those self-made billionaires with humble beginnings. He was born in Hangzhou, located in the south-eastern part of China. He was raised along with an elder brother and a younger sister during the rise of communist China and its isolation from the western regions. His parents were traditional musicians-storytellers and they didn't make enough to even be considered as middle class during those days.

Former US President Richard Nixon's visit to Hangzhou in 1972 improved the situation of tourism in his hometown and Jack wanted to make the most of this opportunity. Jack always wanted to learn English as a kid and he spent his early mornings riding on his bike to a nearby park, giving English tours to foreigners for free. That was how he met a foreign girl who gave him the nickname 'Jack', because she found his name hard to spell.

Jack, after graduating with a bachelor's degree in English, worked as an English teacher at Hangzhou Dianzi University with a pay of $12 a month! Now here comes the part where it gets more interesting — even before he received that degree and became an English teacher. Jack Ma was an extremely lucky bloke who just became a billionaire in a snap, but you wouldn't believe the number of times this man has experienced failure and rejection.

> *Never give up. Today is hard,*
>
> *Tomorrow will be worse,*
>
> *But the day after tomorrow will be sunshine."*
>
> — *Jack Ma*

In his early childhood, Jack Ma failed in his primary school examinations, not once, but twice! He failed thrice during his middle school exams. When applying to universities after his high school, Jack failed the entrance exams thrice, before finally joining Hangzhou Normal University. He even applied and wrote to Harvard University ten times– and got rejected each time. This was only during his education!

During and after his bachelor's degree Jack tried and failed to get a job at a multitude of places. After spending three years to get into a university, Jack failed to land a job after applying 30 times! He recollects in an interview, "When KFC came to China, 24 people went for the job. Twenty-three people were accepted. I was the only guy who wasn't."

He was also one of the 5 applicants to a job in the police force and was the only one rejected after being told, "No, you're no good."

Also, on his entrepreneurial undertakings, Jack Ma went on to fail in two of his initial ventures. But that didn't stop him in any way from dreaming bigger! In one of his interviews, when asked about his rejections, this is what he had to say: "Well, I think we have to get used to it. We're not that good." Overcoming the pain of rejections and treating rejections as opportunities to learn and grow helped Jack Ma succeed.

After finally coming to terms with all his rejections and failures, Jack Ma visited the US in 1995, for a government undertaking project related to the building of highways. It was then that he was first introduced to the internet and computers. Computers were rare in China then, given the high costs associated with them, and the internet was non-existent. The first word he searched on the mosaic browser was 'beer', and it popped out results from different countries, but no sign of China anywhere. He then searched 'China' and not a single result popped out! He decided it was time for China and its people to get on the internet.

Finally, after persuading 17 of his other friends to invest and join him in his new e-commerce startup Alibaba, the company began from his apartment. Initially, Alibaba didn't have a single penny in investment from outside investors, but they later raised $20 million from Softbank and another $5 million from Goldman Sachs in 1999. Building trust among the people of China that an online system of payment and package transfers is safe, was the biggest challenge Jack Ma and Alibaba faced, a challenge that Jack will cherish for his lifetime.

Having started his first successful company at the age of 31 and even after never having written a single line of code or selling something to anyone, Jack Ma runs one of the biggest e-commerce networks in the world. The company went on to grow rapidly, expanding across the world, quickly growing out of its China shell. Only second to Wal-Mart now in terms of sales per year, Alibaba has become the e-commerce giant that Jack Ma envisioned for it.

> "We keep fighting, we keep changing ourselves.
>
> We don't give up."
>
> — *Jack Ma*

What does all this lead to? Believing in yourself, being persistent in the face of adversities and treating rejections and failures as opportunities to propel yourself ahead. That is what Jack Ma's extraordinary life speaks out to the world. This is the story of the exceptionally optimistic and determined entrepreneur who has changed the face of business and internet in China and across the world.

HERO NUMBER 3: **NICK VUJICIC**

> "I was never crippled
>
> Until I lost hope."
>
> — *Nick Vujicic*

Nick Vujicic, born without arms or legs, refuses to let his rare condition confine him to a wheelchair. Born with phocomelia, Nick travels the world inspiring millions with his story.

He plays golf, skydives, swims and surfs. He does not see himself as disabled and has done everything in his power to turn his disadvantage into an advantage. His most recent book, *Unstoppable,* just made the New York Times bestselling list. But despite his current success as an author and public speaker, his journey has not always been an easy ride.

Nick was rejected by his mother after his birth, when she discovered he had no limbs. As a teenager, he was discriminated against, mocked, and insulted simply because he had no legs and hands. Nick in one of his interviews said, "On the morning of my birth, dad was beside her and could see my shoulder had no arm. He nearly fainted and vomited, and the nurse had to take him out of the room. I had phocomelia, no limbs, and there was no medical explanation. It wasn't genetic, and it wasn't thalidomide. They said I would be a vegetable.

My mum said, 'Take him away I don't want to see him.' But my dad comforted her and said, 'He's beautiful.' They took me home, but it took three to four months for my mother to come to terms with it."

Today, Pastor Nick is traveling round the world speaking to millions of people and changing lives. He has turned his limitations into a channel of blessings.

> *"Some injuries heal more quickly*
>
> *If you keep moving."*
>
> — *Nick Vujicic*

Born without limbs, but getting the best out of this life, Nick Vujicic is a powerful motivational speaker who manages to shake his audience to its very core every single time. Having no arms and legs… imagine that for a second! It should be enough for your brain to take you through a series of events regarding how life would be like. Now imagine that this same man can swim, surf, play football, and golf.

> *Having faith, beliefs, and convictions*
>
> *Is a great thing, but your life is measured*
>
> *By the actions you take based upon them."*
>
> — *Nick Vujicic*

Despite all the challenges he had to put up with, Vujicic continues to push his limits and has made a name for himself in teaching others about self-love and confidence in the face of disability and adversity. It is ironic how our mind can paralyze us despite us having full control of our bodies; yet extraordinary what it can offer when unlocked. Nick's story is one that drives chills into my bones each time I read it. If someone without limbs could choose to be happy and strive to be successful in life despite his limitations, then why can't you?

HERO NUMBER 4: **ALBERT EINSTEIN**

> *"Everybody is a genius.*
>
> *But if you judge a fish by its ability to climb a tree,*
>
> *It will live its whole life believing that it is stupid."*
>
> — *Albert Einstein*

Born in 1879, the man that we all know as one of the most brilliant minds to have ever lived was once considered a major failure. In fact, Einstein didn't speak until he was 4 years old. Yes, 4 years old. In 1895, at the age of 16, he failed to pass the examination for entrance into the Swiss Federal Polytechnic School in Zurich.

And while he did graduate from university, he struggled and nearly dropped out, doing very poorly during his studies there. In fact, he was in such dire straits that at the time of his father's death, he considered his son to be a major failure, which left young Einstein completely heartbroken.

"In the middle of difficulty lies

Opportunity."

— *Albert Einstein*

After graduating, he wandered, unsure of what to do with his life. After some time, he ended up taking a job as an insurance salesman, going door to door to sell insurance. Eventually, two years later, he took a job at the patent office as an assistant examiner, evaluating patent applications for a variety of devices.

Of course, this is the same individual who brought us the theory of relativity, with groundbreaking work done in physics and mathematics. He helped us to reach deeper understandings about how the universe works, developing several fundamental, core laws governing physics, won the Nobel Prize in 1921, and created the beginnings of quantum theory.

HERO NUMBER 5: *COLONEL HARLAND SANDERS*

> *"No hours, nor amount of labor,*
> *Nor amount of money would deter me from*
> *Giving the best that there was in me."*
>
> — **Colonel Sanders**

Born in 1890 in Indiana, Colonel Harland Sanders, the founder of Kentucky Fried Chicken (KFC), is famous not only for his chicken recipe, but also his numerous failures in life and in business. At the ripe young age of 5 years old, his father died, leaving only his mother to fend for and support three children, including Harland. While his mother left for days on end, Harland was forced to help take care of his siblings and became a proficient cook during this time, learning how to make bread and vegetables and advancing in his knowledge of cooking and preparing meat by the age of just 7 years old. By 10 years old, he was already working as a farmhand.

In 1902, when Harland was 12 years old, his mother remarried, subjecting the children to an arduous environment that ultimately forced Harland to leave home the following year. By age 14, he began working as a farmhand at another farm in southern Indiana. Sanders worked odd jobs for years, never able to make anything stick. He owned a ferry boat company on the Ohio River, sold tyres in Winchester Kentucky, and later, in 1930, opened a restaurant inside a shell oil company-owned gas station in north Corbin Kentucky where he began serving chicken dishes. He was 40 years old at the time.

In July 1939, he came to own a restaurant and motel which was destroyed by a fire just 4 months later. But it wasn't until 1940 that he began to finalize his so-called "secret" chicken recipe, at the age of 50.

However, in 1942, during the war, he sold his business and subsequently got divorced in 1947.

In 1955, another one of his restaurants failed after an interstate route that led traffic past that restaurant, was changed. That year, with just a $105 social security check to his name, at the age of 65, he set out to sell his franchised chicken model to restaurants across the country. He was famously rejected by 1,009 restaurants before one agreed to his idea. Colonel Harland Sanders died with an estimated net worth of 3.5 million dollars. His company, Kentucky Fried Chicken, has an estimated net worth of 15 billion dollars, as of 2013.

HERO NUMBER 6: **TIMAYA**

"Sometimes it takes a fall

For a man to realize how strong he is."

— *Timaya*

Enitimi Alfred Odom, better known by his stage name Timaya, is a Nigerian singer and songwriter. Born 15 August 1980, he is the founder of South-South hip hop group Dem Mama Soldiers. From a former plantain seller who once lived with a woman older than him in Port-Harcourt, to the huge star we know today, this is the story of a great young man who rose beyond all limitations to become the man he is today.

Timaya ran away from home at the age of 14. The stubborn and opinionated child was the last born in a family of 15 children whose father wanted him to become a banker like he was. But obviously, he had other ideas as he grew up loving entertainment and was not ready to compromise his dream for anything else. Sometimes when there was a show in town, he would sneak out to watch the show and when he came back the next morning, his mother would want to kill him. Timaya, having taken part in a talent audition organized by Hilda Dokubo and her husband and lost, met K-Solo in his studio in Mafoluku Oshodi and would often take a bike from his sister's place in Oshodi to the studio.

They began work on his album, recorded seven raw and uncut demo CDs, and cut 5000 promo CDs without mixing the songs before giving them out to people for free. With a determined mind, he met with Danco Music who offered to buy his master tape for one million naira, after T-Joe and Obaino had offered him 40,000 naira - 45,000 naira. With the new offer of one million naira, he went back to Port Harcourt and spent N190, 000 to buy a power bike and rent an apartment. The rest of the money he spent on secondhand wears as he felt his status needed an upgrade.

According to Timaya, he survived on the mangoes he plucked in the compound after the money was spent. Little did he know his breakthrough was coming! His first breakthrough came when he was paid N150, 000 to perform for students of Federal Polytechnic Nekede, Owerri and since then Timaya has never looked back.

Timaya got rejected several times when he started; he is a true example of a fighter and a strong believer in the grace of God upon his life. Today he is among the highly celebrated and richest musicians in Nigeria and Africa with a net worth of $6.5m.

HERO NUMBER 7: *YINKA AYEFELE*

> *"Accident can take your ability to walk,*
> *But never allow it to take your*
> *Ability to think positively."*
>
> — *Yinka Ayelefe*

There are many sides to living. Yinka Ayelefe, the physically challenged musician, has seen it all. Perhaps not all sides to life, but he has seen many flip sides. A long time ago, he could walk. For 30 of his 52 years, he went everywhere his feet could take him. He could stand, walk, run, jump and do any of the things he needed to with the aid of his feet.

Those were mostly joy-filled years, when he hoped to accomplish many things as a voice-over artiste, broadcaster and budding musician. In the last 22 years, he has been confined to a wheelchair. The years have been difficult, and he must smile through the pain, with undying optimism that he will walk again, even if some people only see the apparent material comfort he has attained.

Following a car crash 22 years ago which damaged his spinal cord, Ayefele is the subject of an engaging spectacular legend. Most surprising of all is that a man in a wheelchair is a source of inspiration and motivation to countless numbers including over 140 employees who call him 'chairman'. His growing enterprise includes a hospitality business, a band, multi-media, and a radio station, Fresh 105.9FM.

No one expected this inexplicable turn of fortunes; from a seemingly hopeless situation to increasing prosperity. Evidently, 'glory to God' is a perpetual phrase on his lips. The ghastly accident that almost took his life occurred on December 12, 1997 along Ibadan –Abeokuta road. The tragic event has since become the defining moment that transformed his life. With the accident came a Midas touch. Everything he touches turns to gold. Today Mr. Ayefele is founder and CEO with hundreds of employers on his payroll even while on a wheelchair.

HERO NUMBER 8: DR INNOCENT CHUKWUMA IFEDIASO

> "Do not despise the little beginnings of life
>
> For in them one builds the character
>
> And strength of the bigger things to come."
>
> — *Dr Innocent Chukwuma Ifediaso*

This success story is about Innocent Chukwuma Ifediaso, a multi-million-dollar Nigerian entrepreneur who went from selling spare parts as far back as 1979, to building a large conglomerate that manufactures motorcycles, tricycles, spare parts, tires, cars, and many other commodities. Innocent, the last of 6 kids, was born in Nnewi, Anambra State, in 1961 to Mr. And Mrs. Chukwuma Mojekwu.

In 1978 after he was done with his secondary school education, Innocent applied to study engineering at the university. He waited for a while to get his admission results before resorting to working at his elder brother's medicine store. When his university application results were finally out, he didn't make the cut, and so couldn't get in that year. While he worked for his brother Gabriel, he realized he had a natural talent for trading, and so moved on to serve Chief Romanus Eze Onwuka, where he learnt a trade.

A year later, in 1979, Innocent left his boss and returned to his brother. He registered a business called Gabros International. The business was funded by his brother to the tune of 3,000 naira ($10; which had a considerably higher value back then) and traded in motorcycle spare parts. With total freedom to run the business his own way, Innocent rented a shop and started purchasing merchandise.

By the end of 1980, Innocent and his elder brother, Gabriel, took a thorough account of everything the medicine store and the spare part business were making, and realized that Gabros International was making 10 times more money than the medicine store. When Innocent personally ventured into motorcycle sales, he realized that most people were importing used motorcycles into Nigeria, and that their prices were high. This prompted him to device a way to bring in brand new motorcycles into the country, at a price far lower than the used motorcycles.

With this goal, he took a trip abroad to see how it was all done. He realized there were four companies bringing in the motorcycles at the time. These were Leventis, Yamaco, Boulous, and CFAO. He noticed that when they imported the motorcycles, they'd bring them in crates, and each crate could only contain one motorcycle, which would take up a lot of space. This meant only 40 crates could be put into a 40-feet container, and upon arrival, the motorcycles would naturally become expensive to buyers.

This insight gave Innocent a great idea. He would purchase the motorcycles overseas and disassemble them before he shipped them. This enabled him ship 200 motorcycles in parts, in one 40-feet container. Upon arrival, he'd reassemble them, and his motorcycles would cost 40% less than his competitors'. This tactic brought down the average cost of a motorcycle from 150,000 naira to 60,000 naira, and subsequently exploded his sales and revenues.

Innocent Chukwuma Ifediaso has gone through lot of setbacks and storms in his life, including rejection, betrayal from friends, and even criticism and lack of support from his own country government. But, this dynamic man refused to throw in the towel. Rather he fought his way to success and today he is celebrated and admired. He is the founder and CEO of a plastic factory in Nigeria, which is now one of the largest in Africa, and a vehicle manufacturing company called Innoson Vehicle Manufacturing (IVM), which manufactures trucks, SUVS, buses, sedans, and even spare parts for the Nigerian Army's fighter jets; the first of its kind in Nigeria.

HERO NUMBER 9: SOICHIRO HONDA

> *"Success represents 1% of your work*
>
> *Which results only from the 99% that is called failure."*
>
> *— Soichiro Honda*

Born in 1906, Soichiro Honda was a Japanese inventor and industrialist who created the automotive empire that bears his name: Honda Motor Company. However, while Honda's company has certainly grown to rival even Toyota, Honda's earliest days were anything but easy. Yet, it was his perseverance and his tenacity to never give up that kept him going and helped him to ultimately succeed.

Without any formal education to his name, at the age of 15 years old, Honda left home and headed for Tokyo to search for work, which he later found at an auto repair shop where he apprenticed and worked for the next 6 years before returning home to open his own automotive shop.

During the great depression, in 1937, at the age of 31 years old, he founded Tōkai Seiki to create piston rings for Toyota. He toiled and labored night and day to create these, but to no avail. With little cash and bleak chances for survival, he had to pawn his wife's ring just to make ends meet. He failed ultimately and was told that the rings didn't meet Toyota's specifications.

However, he refused to give up. He went back to school and continued to search for ways to improve upon his prior designs. Eventually, after two more years of designing and trying, he succeeded and secured a contract with Toyota to create the piston rings.

But shortly thereafter, his factory which he built to manufacture the products was hit by a bomb during World War 2 when a B-29 bomber carpeted the area. After he rebuilt the factory a second time, an earthquake leveled it. But he refused to give up. Instead, he created a motorized bicycle that would become the start of the Honda motorcycle and later the Honda Group Companies.

HERO NUMBER 10: J.K. ROWLING

> *"It is our choices that show what we truly are,*
>
> *Far more than our abilities."*
>
> *— J.K Rowling*

Quite possibly one of the most famous and renowned former failures of our time, J.K. Rowling is the author of the wildly popular *Harry Potter* book series. Born in 1965, she had a tumultuous childhood that included a difficult and oftentimes strained relationship with her father, and dealing with her mother's illness.

In 1982, at the age of 17, she attempted to gain acceptance to Oxford University. She failed and was rejected, instead enrolling at the University of Exeter where she received her Bachelor of Arts in French and classics. After graduating from university, at the age of 21, she moved to London to work for Amnesty International in 1986.

> *"We do not need magic to transform our world.*
>
> *We carry all of the power we need inside ourselves already."*
>
> — *J.K Rowling*

After London, she moved to Manchester with her boyfriend. It was there, in 1990, at the age of 25, while on a 4-hour-delayed train, that the idea of a young wizard popped into her mind. She later stated that it came "fully formed," and all she needed to do was flesh out the details.

However, it was just a few short months after that her mother, Anne, died from multiple sclerosis, leaving her extremely distraught and upset. In the wake of her mother's death, only a few months afterwards, she moved to Porto, in Portugal, to teach English. There, she met a man, got married, got pregnant, and gave birth to her daughter, who was born in 1993.

The relationship was a very strained one, with reports of domestic abuse, resulting in a separation and eventual divorce. With only three chapters of *Harry Potter* completed, at the end of 1993, when she was 28 years old, she moved to Edinburgh to live with her sister.

At that point, she considered herself a major failure. She had failed at just about everything she had ever attempted to do in life. She was diagnosed with clinical depression and was suicidal. Two years later, in 1995, five years after the initial idea had come to her, she managed to finish the manuscript for *Harry Potter and the Sorcerer's Stone*. She located an agent, but after one year of trying to get it published, all 12 major publishing houses had rejected her book.

It wasn't until 1996, when a small literary house in London named Bloomsbury, gave the green light and a very small advance of £1500, only at the behest of the owner's daughter, that the book was published. In 1997, seven years after the initial idea for the young wizard, the first

Harry Potter book was published. By 2004, Rowling had become the first author to become a billionaire through book writing, according to *Forbes*.

HERO NUMBER 11: *CURTIS JACKSON A.K.A. 50-CENT*

> "Sunny days wouldn't be special,
>
> If it wasn't for rain. Joy wouldn't feel so good
>
> If it wasn't for pain."
>
> — *50 Cents*

Born in 1975, in Queens, New York, Curtis Jackson, professionally known as 50 Cent, had a tumultuous past and a precarious upbringing. Growing up in poverty isn't easy on anyone, especially in the projects in New York's roughest neighborhoods. Not only were drugs and crime all around him, but his own birth mother, Sabrina, was a drug dealer. When he was just 8 years old, his mother, however, died in what has been coined a "mysterious" fire. His father left, leaving only his grandmother to help raise young Curtis, who started dealing drugs at the age of 12 during what has been labeled the "crack epidemic," in the 1980's.

In 1994, at the age of 19, after a string of run-ins with the cops and a subsequent arrest for possession of drugs and a firearm, he was sentenced to serve 3 to 9 years in prison but was instead sent to a boot camp where he spent just 6 months, earning his GED in the meantime. It was after his release that he adopted the name 50 Cent as a moniker for change, naming himself after a local bank robber by the same name. He states that he chose that name "because it says everything I want it to say. I'm the same kind of person 50 Cent was. I provide for myself by any means."

In 2000, he was infamously shot 9 times at close range by an assailant outside his grandmother's home and left for dead. While in the hospital, he signed a deal with Columbia Records, but was subsequently dropped from that label and even blacklisted within the recording industry due to a song entitled, "Ghetto Quran," forcing him to go to Canada to record over 30 songs and release a mixtape.

In 2002, Eminem heard his song, "Guess Who's Back?" and ultimately signed him to his label, Shady Records. He was coached by both Eminem and Dr. Dre, and released his first studio album, *Get Rich or Die Trying*, which later went 6-times platinum in the United States. Curtis Jackson has since become one of the world's most famous rappers, as well as an actor and an entrepreneur.

To me, he is a big inspiration, and tells another great story about a guy who started from the bottom and worked his way to the top. 50 Cent's net worth is currently estimated to be $20 million. What a journey.

HERO NUMBER 12: **HENRY FORD**

"Obstacles are those frightful things you see

When you take your eyes off your goal."

— *Henry Ford*

Born in Greenfield Township, Michigan, in 1863, Henry Ford was the industrialist who started Ford Motor Company, which has been one of the most profitable automotive companies in the world over the years, making him into one of the richest and most famous individuals on the planet. However, while Ford celebrated many successes later in life, he also failed often in his earlier years.

In 1891 when Ford was 28 years old he decided to become an engineer, working for the Edison Illuminating Company and earning a promotion in 1893 at the age of 30, to chief engineer. It was around this time he started experimenting with gasoline engines. However, it wasn't until 1898, when Ford was 35 years old, that he designed and built a self-propelled vehicle which he showed off to people, winning the backing of William H. Murphy, who, at the time, was a lumber baron in Detroit. Subsequently, Ford founded the Detroit Automobile Company a year later in 1899.

In 1901, however, that company failed after an inability to pay back a loan to the Dodge Brothers and due to inefficiencies in the design of the vehicle; the company ceased operations, dealing a stealthy blow to Ford. However, subsequently, Ford convinced one of his partners to give him another chance. With mounting pressure, it was agreed that he would try again. But after disagreements, this venture also flopped.

In 1903, Ford gave it one final shot. At the age of 40, after two separate failures, he tried again, incorporating the Ford Motor Company. Even after the failures, Ford found an unconventional backer and made him agree not to meddle in the business. He found this in Alexander Y. Malcolmson, a Scottish immigrant who had made his fortune in the coal industry. Afterwards, what transpired is one of the most famous stories of an individual who went from failure to success in the grandest way.

The Ford name is synonymous with the automobile. In fact, while the assembly line existed prior to Ford's arrival on the scene, so to speak, he created a car that was affordable by the everyday family, helping to develop what was to become the largest boon in the automotive industry, with cars everywhere.

HERO NUMBER 13: **KATY PERRY**

> *"I've lived such a great, fantastic life already,*
>
> *But there's still so much more."*
>
> *— Katy Perry*

Born in 1984 in Santa Barbara, California, Katy Perry is an American singer and songwriter best known for her hit, "I Kissed a Girl". Perry experienced a seemingly sudden rise to fame. But did she really? In fact, Perry experienced numerous heart-wrenching failures on the path towards stardom before she ever became a household name.

In her childhood, her family faced severe struggles, oftentimes living in poverty, having to use food stamps just to get by, which had a big impact on Perry's upbringing. From an early age, she realized that things weren't easily obtained, and that she would have to work hard for them, something that clearly stuck with her through the failures.

Growing up, Perry and her siblings listened to gospel music often. At the age of 13, she was gifted a guitar, and shortly thereafter she began performing the songs that she wrote using that very guitar. However, she was far from famous. In fact, fame was going to elude her for quite some time.

In 1999, at the age of 15, she dropped out of high school after completing her GED to pursue music full time. She moved to Tennessee where she signed with Red Hill Records and debuted a gospel record entitled, *Katy Hudson* in March 2001 at the age of 17. It sold only 200 copies before the label ceased its operations a few months later.

In 2004, at the age of 20, she signed with another label called Java, which was associated with the Island Def Jam music group, to work on her solo record. However, after Def Jam dropped Java, the record was shelved. Afterwards, Perry signed with Columbia Records, and recorded new music over the next two years. But before the record was completed, she was dropped from that label as well. However, her big break came in 2007 when she signed with Capitol Records. In 2008, when she released the would-be-hit song, "I Kissed a Girl", Perry was 24 years old. What seemed like an overnight success took 9 years to accomplish, from the time that she dropped out of high school.

HERO NUMBER 14: **HOWARD SCHULTZ**

> *"I am convinced that most people can*
> *Achieve their dreams and beyond if they have*
> *The determination to keep trying."*
>
> *— Howard Schultz*

Howard Schultz, the man behind one of the largest and most successful coffee companies in the world, and currently 2020 independent presidential candidate has lived a rags-to-riches story, starting off poor and creating a $3 billion fortune as well as more than 300,000 jobs.

Born in 1953, Howard Schultz is the famous American entrepreneur behind the wildly successful coffee company, Starbucks. However, his early life, like many other famous people who failed at first, started off in extreme poverty, growing up in Canarsie, part of the New York City housing projects. In 1975, he graduated with a bachelor's in arts from the Northern Michigan University, which he attended on a sports scholarship.

After graduation, Schultz headed to Xerox Corporation and he was quickly promoted to become a full sales representative. After Xerox, in 1979, at the age of 24, he headed to a Swedish coffeemaker called Hammerplast as the general manager. It was a small company comprising just 20 employees. However, it was the company's client, Starbucks that led him on the next leg of his journey in life.

In 1982, at the age of 29, he joined Starbucks, after being so impressed with the company, as their director of marketing. A year later, in 1983, after a trip to Italy, Schultz, realizing the prevalence of the coffee culture there and the country's 200,000 coffee bars, convinced the owners of Starbucks to roll out the concept across the company's stores. Previously, they just sold coffee beans and not actual coffee drinks.

While the owners resisted at first, he was persistent and was able to open a coffee shop in one of the new stores in Seattle, which debuted in 1984. It was an instant success. But the owners didn't want to continue with the concept. They didn't want Starbucks to get too big. In 1985, Schultz left Starbucks to open his own coffee bar, naming it Giornale, Italian for 'the newspaper.'

However, the story clearly didn't end there. After two years, Schultz had achieved great success with his coffee shop, but he was thinking even bigger. He proposed buying the Starbucks Company, which at the time carried a hefty price tag, so he needed help with the transaction. Attempting to raise the capital to purchase the company, Schultz famously stated that he "was turned down by 217 of the 242 investors I initially talked to. You have to have a tremendous belief in what you're doing and just persevere."

HERO NUMBER 15: LINDA IKEJI

"Your life can change for the better in an instant and that instant can last forever. Just remember to always hold on to God. He's watching. He's seeing your struggles and one day, he'll hold your hands and never let go."

— *Linda Ikeji*

Linda Ikeji was born Linda Ifeoma Ikeji in 1980. She is the second of seven children born to parents from Nkwerre in the Southeastern state of Imo, Nigeria. Like many other families from this region, Linda was raised in a poor Christian home that went through its fair share of poverty. At the young age of 10, she had already begun writing short fictional stories as a hobby. Added to her knack for storytelling, she loved to report on the news and was fascinated by interviews.

This prompted her to pursue a degree in Mass Communication at the University of Lagos. Unfortunately for her, she was instead admitted to study English Language. She began university at the age of 19 and due to her parent's financial instability, she had to struggle and work to support herself financially. She worked different jobs as a waitress, an usher at occasions, a bartender, and a model.

Upon the completion of her university education, Linda set up her own modeling agency called Black Dove Communications, but the business was not as profitable as she hoped and later it closed, but Linda refused to give in to defeat and rather continued to craft out better ways to change her life. As you already know, not all success stories are smooth, and Linda's is not an exception. Her "sudden" rise to fame and riches as some would see it, was never sudden. Her journey, like every other hero in this book, was full of difficulties, financial instability and of course as a beautiful young girl, distractions. But it's amazing how she struggled through with determination and focus, walking tall through it all.

She started blogging in November 2006, at a time when internet access was least pronounced in Nigeria and only a few people blogged about their personal lives and their families. She often tells the story of how she used to borrow money to go to the cybercafé to blog. That kicked off the beginning of the acclaimed and successful Linda Ikeji blog. Since its official inception in 2007, Linda Ikeji Blog has become a well-known blog all around Africa. Starting first as a gossip blog which was then first of its kind in Nigeria, it has grown to become the centerpiece of entertainment, covering news and events happening in and around Africa and even beyond.

Through dedication, perseverance and focus, this young and extraordinary young woman from Nigeria has crafted a name for herself and her family and touched the lives of hundreds of young females in the country, giving them start-up capital to venture into any trade of their choice. Today she is worth more than $30 million dollars.

If you carefully read the stories of these men and women, you will see just three things common with each of them and these are determination, persistence and a unique vision and goal that they wanted to fulfill and so nothing could stop them. This is just a summary of what these men and women went through to become the great men and women we celebrate and admire today. Some of them even went through secret pains that they kept to themselves alone and refused to share with anybody.

I share this with you to show you that you are not the first person on this road, and you won't be the last. So, it's your choice to either give in or decide to fight till you win. It is said that quitters never win and winners never quit. Which are you?

I have had my own share of tough times in life. I grew up in a poor home. My dad was a police officer back when police officers in Nigeria were paid less than $20 per month as salary and my mother was a trader. Here they were with five children, four boys and a girl. We lived in one 10x 12 room, all seven of us. At age 16, I had started catering for myself even while my dad was alive because I did not want to be a burden to him. I decided to reduce his burden and help myself.

I remember the days of high school, when I close from school each day, I would enter the rain forest to cut firewood and take it on a wheel barrow to sell in the market for less than 12 cent. This I would do for three weeks before I could raise some money to buy myself clothes and shoes and support my siblings. After some time, the business stopped yielding income for me. At age 16, I started working in a cocoa exporting company, not as a corporate staff, but as a loader. Every night, I would join the rest of the older boys who had well-developed muscles and carry 156-170lbs of cocoa on my neck in a bag, and walk up inside the lorry to load it. For each bag I was paid 1 dollar.

Those were some of the most painful moments of my life as a teenager. At the weekend when there were no trucks to load, I would take my wheel barrow and go help people in the market carry their goods to the motor park, all for peanuts. I would also hawk vegetables on my head around the local community. As if that was not enough, after I gained admission into the university, my father died of high blood pressure, leaving me, my four younger siblings and my poor mum alone in a world where no one cared, with no money, savings or investment.

> *"Until you have gone without food for weeks,*
>
> *You will never value the privilege of having*
>
> *What-a-burger."*
>
> *— Great Igwe*

Even till now, the death of my father is still the worst event of my life. I remember calling my mum from school and telling her I wanted to drop out of school, so I could find work and help sponsor my younger siblings in school since no uncles or aunties were going to help me in school. And, my mum said "Son, no."

I was faced with confusion and felt like taking my own life. I had no food, no clothes, not even a place to stay in school, and no money for school fees. But I rose up one morning and decided I would not let my circumstance decide my fate in life but rather I would decide my own fate. I started doing all sorts of little jobs in school to raise my school fees. I remember falling from a two-story building while I was taking bricks to the builders upstairs. The scars from the fall is still boldly seen in my body.

It was a painful season but very rewarding. Even when I migrated to the United States, it was tough, so tough that it came a point when I felt like going back. I came into the country with only $20 and while I was still figuring myself, I took ill and spent 7days at the hospital with no family around to hold on to during this bitter moments. Few month later after I came out from the hospital, my relationship with a woman I was engage to ended. And I must confess it was so painful because I loved the lady so much. It was in this trying time of my life that I learnt the hardest lessons of life. It made me responsible, mature, courageous, and more selfless. Above all, it taught me life lessons I never learnt in the classroom.

These lessons are the principles that have shaped my life and made me the man I am today. I have experienced betrayals from my uncles, aunties and even pastor. But I stood strong, having faith in Him who created the heavens and the earth and allowing His will for my life to gradually unfold. Today the story is different. I look back at those years and I celebrate them because they brought forth the man I am today. If I can, then you can too.

One of the saddest mistakes a person can make is to believe that he/she cannot make it. I want to tell you that the only thing you cannot do, is what you have not attempted to do. If you will dare it, you will do it. Develop a conviction in your mind that, if somebody else can do it, I can do it too. Even better. People who have done or are doing it do not have 6 eyes, 7 ears, 8 mouths, 9 brains etc. Nope!!!

You have all that the greatest of men have. Please! Never, ever look down on yourself. You may not be born with a silver spoon, but in your hand lies a tool to carve out for yourself a golden one. It might seem as if things are not taking the expected shape. Keep on keeping on. When it seems that God is coming too late, He's coming in a big way. Just decide what you want to be and don't settle for anything less. Believe that you can live your dream and then work towards your goal. Be relentless in your pursuit and always think like a champion. All improvement in your life begins with an improvement in your mental pictures.

It's never too late to be what you might have been. Okay, now if you can't be a sun, then be a star. Just make sure you become something better than good. If others, these men and women above, have done it, you too can do it. Even if no one has ever done it, then be the first in history to do it. You can do it. You can succeed. You can be truly great. You can break records. You can...

Not Like the Rest

Show the world you are not like the rest. Push yourself to become your very best. Most people accept the average existence handed down to them by generations of uninspired role models. Make sure in your family, in your circle, it stops with you! You are different, and you will show everyone that greatness, happiness and abundance are not only possible, they are very achievable! Don't talk about it. Show everyone when you make it.

Most people give up too easily. Most people are ready to throw in the towel when things get tough. Most people stop chasing their dreams because of fear. Most people. Not you! You never give up when times get tough. You will keep on going even if the odds are stacked against you. That's what makes you special! That's what makes you a champion! I've never heard of a champion giving up when times get tough. Champions keep on going until they get the victory. That's a champion's mindset.

Not everyone becomes a champion, only those with a burning desire and a huge passion for what they do, are the ones who get the title. There are lots of people who started with nothing but ended up with everything. If they can do it, why can't you? You just must think like a champion, train like a champion and be a champion! If you must, fake it until you make it!

A lot of people talk about how they're going to succeed. They talk, not work. It's easier to talk about what you are going to do, than do it. No one became successful by doing things the easy way. No one became successful by talking and wishing only without working. People became successful by doing! Actions they say speak louder than words! If you don't work for what you want, you will end up with something that you don't want. If you don't work for what you want, you will most likely work for someone who did what you did not want to work for.

Most people don't go after what they want because of fear of success or fear of failure. Remember that you only get one chance at life, make sure it's unforgettable! You're not like the rest. The champion says: "I can!" The champion says: "I will." The champion doesn't care if you call it impossible for the champion knows nothing is impossible! The champion doesn't care for your hate cause the champion is working on becoming great. You are the captain of your fate, the master of your destination, the boss of your dreams, the king of your goals. Get out there and create your own legacy.

Chapter Eleven

YOU MATTER

A song writer said, and I quote; "Learning to love yourself is the greatest love of all." That is a very powerful statement. The enemy can take away your properties but never allow the enemy take away your ability to see good in yourself. You are worth more than you can ever imagine. Despite whatever circumstances of life you might be going through, or the mistakes of the past. The Trust of the matter is that the world is incomplete without you. The world needs you.

Knowing you matter isn't about being self-absorbed or narcissistic. Shot out that voice inside you that keeps telling you are not worthy, not important. That negative voice that says you are a failure and would never become anything useful in your life because of the mistakes you made I'm the past. Or that you would not amount to anything because of the economic level of your family or parents. It time to open your heart to that positive Holy Spirit voice saying you are saved. Saying you are worth dying for. Saying you are loved and a champion. God is not done with you.

How Knowing You Are Significant Can Change Your Life

Knowing that you are important, precious and matter despite what you are going through, is proper self-esteem. It's seeing and understanding your inherent value as a human being. God created humans with value and glory that surpassed the angels. Knowing that you matter is only second to knowing that you're loved. It matters so much your life depends on it.

When people feel like they don't matter they get depressed and withdraw. Isolation and depression are miserable company to keep. Misery drives people to self-harm and sometimes suicide. The Bible says He created us just a little lower than Himself. If that wasn't enough when humanity fell from that glory God got it back for us through Jesus.

Bad things they say also happens to good people. There is an old African proverb that says the rain falls on the roof of both the evil and good people. It happens to the best of us: Sometimes it seems like our lives don't matter. Whether you are in the depths of depression or have survived an assault on who you are, or even if you are just having a really bad day, sometimes it seems like, "Your life doesn't matter." However: That thought is wrong. Your life does matter. If you are alive, your life matters. No matter the hurts, the bruises and shame, the truth is that the cross had made you flawless.

Learn from Yesterday,

Live for today and hope for Tomorrow. **Bishop Harry Jackson Jr**

Here are some reason why I say you do matter!

- ➢ Everything you see in the world has a lesson to teach you.
- ➢ Every day that you are alive you are acquiring experience and knowledge.
- ➢ Using your money for charitable purposes makes your work and money meaningful.

- You have the ability to use your resources to produce more than is given to you.

- You can set an example of gracious conduct.

- The soul inside you never grows weary; it allows you to continue on even when you are physically and emotionally tired.

- The real you is the inner you, and when you are living with the real you, your life takes on greater meaning.

- Every year on your birthday, the special energy invested in you at birth is present.

- The Pain you experience can be transformed into growth.

- Ambition and creativity are lifelong journeys, so your life matters regardless of your age.

- Every stage of life has its inherent strengths. The stage of life you are in right now is meaningful even if it feels like a slump.

- You are a partner in the creation of the world. You co-create reality with the Universe.

- You have the power to shape your future.

- The good things you do today have perpetual effects.

- Your joy has a cosmic impact.

- There is a part of you that has never been wounded — and can never be wounded.

- Some of the little things you do in life are more important than the big things.

- The journey of your life is more important than your material accomplishments.

- You might not think you are a leader, but everyone has the ability to influence another person positively.
- You are a link in a long historical chain.
- You can recognize the extraordinary within the ordinary.
- Your life is a miracle, an actual miracle.
- You are inherently good. Your inner self is inherently good. Every person has an inherently beautiful inner self.
- Your life matters because you yearn for something better.
- Your life matters because you care enough to regret your mistakes.
- Regardless of how lonely you feel, you are never alone.
- Your life matters because your birth is God saying, you matter.
- . The world would be different if you were not born.
- You have a unique role to play in the grand scheme of things.
- You have a contribution to make to the world, even if you're not sure what it is.
- You were chosen to be born and to live in this world.
- The small things you do have a bigger positive effect than you know.
- You have said and will say again kind words that made somebody's day.
- You might save someone's life one day.
- You might have already saved someone's life without even knowing it.
- You have many things to accomplish.

- You'd be missed by others if you weren't around, even if you don't think so.

- There are things you've learned that you need to teach.

- Nobody can look out at life with exactly the same eyes as you do.

- You have the ability to choose, and that is a gift.

- You can rectify mistakes by approaching the same situations in better ways in the future.

- You can inspire someone who feels broken.

- You can experience the satisfaction of doing something difficult.

- The soul that lives in your body is yours and only yours, and was put in your body for a reason.

- Your body is a channel for your soul.

- Your potential for growth is unlimited.

- People might have told you that you are worthless, but they are wrong.

- Every morning is an opportunity to renew your connection to your soul.

- Every night is an opportunity to take stock of the day and plan for a better tomorrow.

- Your cells are constantly regenerating, which means that at the cellular level you are always changing and progressing.

Do you know you are Valuable?

Would the world be any different if you weren't born? Do you wake up in the morning feeling like you have an important role to play in the grand scheme of things? Most of us grow up in a world where life is dispensable, where our individual contributions go unrecognized, where there is no real sense that life – ours or anyone's – is significant or meaningful.

At the root of this restlessness and discontent is the deep-seated conviction that "I Don't Matter." A belief that if I were to show up someplace or not, or make some kind of contribution or not, it would not fundamentally affect the world or the people that live in it. Think about that for a minute. If you don't feel like you make a difference in the world, how excited can you be about the things you do and the choices you make? When you wake up in the morning and you feel like what you do that day doesn't matter anyway, how committed or passionate can you be?

This means you are absolutely necessary. You are indispensable to God's vision of the world, chosen to fulfill a mission in this world that you and only you can accomplish like musical notes in the grand Divine composition, each of us has our unique music to play. Few months ago, I received an email from one of my Facebook followers, who read this book. Here is what she wrote on her email.

I am a 33-year-old executive—very successful and accomplished; admired and respected. Yet beneath this fine veneer lies a woman in shreds. You see, my joy and self-esteem was wrecked years ago when my husband abused me physically, emotionally and daily reminded me how ugly I was and how fat I'm. He made me lost my self-worth to the point of considering suicide. Every day of my life is essentially a struggle against suicide. I felt no self-value, actually no self at all. I am a sum of my parts, and my value is based on how others value me. I have tried many therapies but essentially have remained the same. Intimacy doesn't work in my life, relationships are either unhealthy or nonexistent.

"In order to compensate for this deep void and lack, what I have done, as do people in this situation, I have become super ambitious and hyper productive in order to create some semblance of outer control and self-worth in place of no inner control. It helps distract me somewhat and helps get me through the day, but it doesn't really change anything. Inside I'm a wreck, and every day, sometimes every moment, is another struggle of self-acceptance and value.

"I had long given up hope and resigned myself to this life of misery. But then a miracle happened. Someone gave me the book "Walking Tall in Tough Times". I am Jewish but non-observant, and I was glancing through the book with a measure of skepticism until a line jumped out at me and struck me like a thunderbolt, like a silver bullet between the eyes:

"The line said: 'Birth Is God saying that you matter.' I read it again. 'Birth Is God Saying You Matter.' I read it over and over at least 20 times. And I will continue to read it every day of my entire life.

"I suddenly realized, after 33years, that no matter what my ex-husband had told me, no matter his abuse, and demoralization of my person, saying I was too fat, an accident and a source of misery in his lives and not attractive. No matter how the society tells me that I'm just a statistic in someone's balance sheet, that my value is measured in buying power, productivity, looks, youth, contacts, and money. None of their opinion matters because I matter to the One who matters most. To God, who created me and said, 'I want you on this Earth. I need you.

"The mere fact that I was born, that I exist, regardless of my mood, my performance level, the mere fact that I am here is a vote of confidence from God that I am indispensable, absolutely necessary, and irreplaceable. No one can replace me. I matter. I truly matter.

"Do you know how that made me feel? That I have permission to matter. I am commanded to matter. "So though I still have many years to heal, now, for the first time in my life, I have hope. And I know what I need to do. I need to create bypass surgery to bypass the infected arteries that my ex-husband gave me when they touched me, criticized me, hit me, for the first time, and reconnect to that first, pure, innocent moment of birth, when God said you matter, you are indispensable. "So thank you for giving me back my life."

This young lady email, left me in tears for some time. It is a letter that touched my heart. I grew up in a very healthy home and was nurtured and made to feel valuable. But hearing the heart-wrenching story from a woman who did not have that luxury from her own husband, I was challenged to ask myself: "Do I matter because my parents valued me and because of my achievements, or do I matter in a more permanent and eternal way?"

I began to pose this question to some of my social media followers across the country – and I ask you, dear reader, the same: Do you think that you really matter? The knee-jerk response is usually: Of course I matter – I feel that I am important. My family, friends and work colleagues value me. But let me rephrase the question: Would it make a difference if you were never born? Remember, before you were born, it would not be a catastrophe if you did not appear; no one would miss you because no one was expecting you.

Of course, we can justify our existence once we are born. But does our existence have any merit beyond our justifications? The only absolute reason why you truly matter is because you were chosen by God to come to this world. Yes, you matter, not because you think you are important, or because others tell you that you are, or because of your buying power, monetary value, looks, performance or productivity level. But because God put you here. You are an indispensable musical note. Irreplaceable. Period. The world would be different if you were not here or if you do not fulfill your calling. You have been allotted a certain section of this globe, with certain talents; people you will meet; experiences you will have; places you will go; objects you will obtain – all are allocated to you in order for you to transform them, to leave them differently from how you found them. And this change lives forever.

When you know that you and your contribution are crucial,

It infuses all that you do with a compelling sense of urgency .

Andrew Wommack

I believe that this simple and clear message is preventive medicine for much of the tragedy and suffering that plague our world today-the shootings, the hatred, the suicides and depression, the wars. We need to reach to every person, to every child, every parent, every educator, every leader, with the message: You matter. Your life and what you do with it matters. You are indispensable to the development of our Nation, State, and local community, But most importantly, to God and to this world at large.

It's also important for you to show the people that you meets each day, that they matter and are important. Not just your family relatives or your spouse. You also need to intentionally show to the stranger you meet on the road that he/she is valuable and important irrespective of their jobs or situations of living. Be it the janitor, taxi driver, Uber/Lyft driver, Plumber, Waiter, Gateman, Security or Nanny. The way and manner you speak to people and regard them, goes a long way to show your personality and character.

We all want people to treat us with respect and value no matter what. The people in your life and around you, want that same validation. In fact, every single person you will ever meet shares this common desire. They want to know they matter. They want to feel that sense of significance and value. A sense of significance and value, is a universal human need. First, you need to fully accept that you matter, and then it's incumbent on you to pass this message along. Would the people in your life can answer, "Yes" to the following questions:

- Do you see me?
- Do you hear me?
- Do you care about me?
- Do I matter to you?

When I think of people who made the biggest impact in my life, it was not their expertise or accomplishments that provided me with the direction, guidance and reassurance I needed to accomplish my goals. It was their sincere belief in me. They let me know through their words and actions that I mattered.

The measure of a life is not what that life accomplishes,

but rather the impact that life has on others.

- Jackie Robinson

Here are The 12 Important things to do in other to ensure a "Yes" every time you encounter or interact with someone significant or yet-to-be significant in your life.

1. See Them

In the movie "Avatar," the Na'vi greeted one another with the phrase, "I see you."It means you have opened your mind and heart to them and are fully present. Though you may know them well, you're as interested as you were the first time you met them. One way to let people know you see them is to begin or end sentences with the word "you."

- I hear you.
- I notice the way you...
- I understand you.
- I appreciate you.
- It was great to spend time with you
- I couldn't have done it without you
- You made my day
- You are a dear friend

Sure, you may say these already to your loved ones or good friends. But how often do you say them to people to whom you aren't as close? Do you say these words to students at school, colleagues at work, a crossing guard, a receptionist or a stranger you pass on the street?

2. Acknowledge Everyone

When you acknowledge someone, you recognize their value and importance. How about starting the day with a "Good Morning" email or Tweet? Or smiling at each and every co-workers as you pass by them in the office? Or reaching out to a new acquaintance you see in a crowd or bump into in the groceries store or shopping mall? Go out of your way to acknowledge people. Make an effort to "see them". Like the Na'vi in the movie Avatar, who greeted one another with the phrase "I see you" as a belief and acknowledgment there is something marvelous in everyone you meet.

3. Listen with Interest

More and more I've come to understand that listening is one of the most important things we can do for one another.... It can often be our greatest gift. Whether that person is speaking or playing or dancing, building or singing or painting, if we care, we can listen. "Listening means more than quietly nodding your head while waiting your turn to speak again. It means opening your ears and heart and making the other person the sole focus of your attention. Often, this is all someone needs from you.

4. Ask Mattering not Matter-of-Fact Questions

Question are a window into our minds and intentions. We show people how much they matter by the kind of questions we ask. How important do these questions make you feel?

- What rocked your world today?
- Who's world did you rock today?
- How can I make your day?
- What can I do to make it better?

5. Be Present

The ultimate present you can give to a love one, is your presence. How many times have you been in a conversation with someone, and you know their mind is in another place? How many times have you felt "unnoticed" when someone was looking right at you? You do not have to be available for everyone in every moment ... but when you have someone's time and attention; honor it with your presence. Really make that person the center of your attention and experience, even if only for a few minutes. It does wonders in the mattering department of our social lives!

6. Believe in Them

All you really need is one person to show you the epiphany of your own power and you're off to the highest sky. If you can hand people the key to their own power, the human spirit is so receptive...if you open doors for people at a crucial moment, you are educating them in the best sense. You are teaching them to open doors for themselves."

When we believe in others and encourage them to believe in themselves, we hand them the key to their own power. We help them stretch their thinking, envision success, and open the door to their true potential. Words are contagious. Hopeful words infect people with energy and enthusiasm. Cynical words unleash energy-sucking negativity, doubt and fear. The words we speak to others may be the catalyst that sends someone into an emotional tailspin or the spark that spurs him to great achievements - by sparking the belief that he can.

7. Deliver Happiness

Cynicism sucks. It sucks the life out of work, business, and people. Life and work is hard enough and it is easy to get into situations that tear us down. People want and need to be inspired. When people are inspired, they are lifted above these kinds of circumstances and allowed to see the upside of what they can achieve or become. If you can be the one who inspires them, by encouragement or modeling, you've helped them and you matter!

8. Talk about Others

No one likes the person in the family, at work, or at the party who only talks about themselves, their interests, their accomplishments and their importance, right? You become far more interesting and important when you talk about the exciting things other people are doing, trying, creating, writing, and sharing. Doing so gives you the opportunity to make a lot of new friends and establish yourself as someone who is always learning and growing from others. Now, that's an accomplishment worth talking about.

9. Offer Hope

At every moment of the day, we are either making the world a better place or making it worse. Our thoughts spread out and become contagious, either positively infecting others or unleashing a plague of negativity, doubt or fear. We have the power to help lift someone up or to bring them down. How we interact with those we meet, may be the catalyst that sets someone into an emotional tailspin or the spark that provides them with encouragement and hope for a better day… or maybe even a better life.

10. Sweat the Small Stuff

Today I heard from a friend. It was a simple text message asking how I was doing followed by it mattered. It doesn't take much to make someone's day. It could be a smile, wink, or tweet. It could be an email of praise or a pat on the back for encouragement. Or, a call to say, "hi – how you doing? You were on my mind. Almost always, it's something small that makes a big difference. So, do sweat the small stuff.

11. Tell the people in your life how you feel about them

If it doesn't come natural to you, all the more reason to do it more often. It will begin to feel natural soon. Of course, "You matter" is what everyone wants to hear, but other phrases work just as well: "I'm happy to see you. You mean so much to me. You're contribution to the team is immeasurable. I so appreciate you." The language of mattering is universal; no translation necessary. Tell people and tell them often how much they matter!

12. Choose 2 Matter

Mattering is a choice. Give yourself that option every day. It doesn't matter how you do it- it only matters that you do it. You can say it, write it, tweet it, or deliver the message in person. Make the choice every day to tell, offer, thank, encourage, inspire, and let others know you notice and believe in them. It could be and often will be the most powerful thing you do all day. Is mattering on your to do list? I'll leave you with this final thought and challenge.

• Can you imagine what kind of world we can create by each of us knowing we matter, believing in ourselves and supporting one another?

• Can you imagine how actions you take today, could make a difference in some one's life tomorrow? And that ripple would last for generations?

I like you to remember always that you matter and that you are significant. Your value and relevance doesn't come from or what you do. Neither is you value in life based on your charisma, Political affiliation, Educational qualifications or your financial level and connection. Your value in life is based upon the fact that Jesus died for you. The kings of kings and the Lord of lords gave His precious life for your redemption. You are a special product that cannot be bought by money. And even if you were the only sinner in the world, Jesus would have still died for you. This is why you are special and significant regardless of your present circumstance. The scripture says in Zechariah 2:8; *For thus says the Lord of host, after glory He has sent me against the nations which plunder you, for he who touches you touches the apple of His eyes. (NKJV).*

Your circumstance doesn't define who you are.

It's not uncommon for people to view what has happened to them in life as part of their very being. Lost your job, and now you are a loser? Lashed out at a friend or family member in anger, and now you are a jerk? Had too much to drink or eat, and now you are a lush or lack willpower? Look at the different circumstances you have been in and consider the self-talk you use to connect who you are with what has happened. It isn't always negative, either; let's say you won an event and you are intelligent for doing so, or that you got the opportunity to pursue a dream vacation or job and you are smart as a result. In almost all cases, people take the situation—what has actually happened—and associate who they are and how they describe themselves with that situation.

> *Sometimes pain is the necessary catalyst for a change*
>
> *And new beginning.*
>
> **- Great Igwe**

This is why parental experts talk about the danger in telling a child who has done well on a test "you are a smart boy/girl" or one who has behaved well in the grocery store for an hour-long shopping spree "you are a good girl/boy". The behavior or incident does not define the person. Yes, the child may have behaved well during that shopping trip, but the trip alone does not define the child as "good". Nor does having a meltdown during that same shopping trip define the child as "bad". The child is inside the situation, not defined by it.

The problem with defining yourself by what happens to you is that life is more random than we'd like to think. Yes, sometimes the person who studies hard or networks well or works all hours succeeds in a way that someone who isn't putting in the effort does not. However, as much as you may not like to admit it, there are also people who don't put in a lot of effort and are naturally talented in a certain way, connected to the right people, or simply in the right place at the right time. Controlling what happens to you is not as easy as it may sound.

Does this mean you don't work hard? You don't take care walking through dark alleys in the middle of the night, and you don't do your best whenever possible? Of course not! You are wired with smarts and positive traits, and each and every person should use them to their best advantage.

What it does mean is that in order to build your personal confidence and move through life in an unshakeable manner, no matter what the outward circumstances may be, you have to learn to start separating who you are and how you think about yourself from what happens to you, good or bad. People who are super smart and talented, and even well networked and liked, get laid off. Someone who is devoted to health and wellness and takes good care of their physical body gets sick. A person who is faithful and loving toward their spouse can be cheated upon. Being a "good" person doesn't mean that only good things will happen to you.

It's important to develop an air of objectivity, and to learn to step back from what happens and observe it as an outsider. Think about a good friend of yours who learns they are getting laid off from a job they have been committed to for years. You likely wouldn't say, as a first response, "Wow! What stupid thing did you do to be chosen for the layoff?" Instead, you'd defend your friend: "Man, I can't believe you got caught up in this.

You were one of their best, most dedicated employees for years. I'm sorry this happened to you." When it isn't you, you can remain detached and positive but when the same event happens to you, you turn inward to figure out where you messed up and to berate yourself over staying too long at the job, not seeing the writing on the wall, speaking out when you shouldn't have at that meeting, not working long enough or working too long, etc., etc. In fact, the ways in which you beat up on yourself are probably endless.

It's time to start treating yourself like you'd treat a good friend and separating who you are from what happens to you. In order to do this, you have to first admit to your own humanity. People make mistakes. People have 20/20 vision when they're looking back on choices they have made. Most people make the best decisions in the moment with the information they have, the tools they have to work with, and the state of mind they are in.

So no matter what's happened to you, it's time to build confidence back and realize you are not your circumstances. Stand outside the fire and look in. Consider some of the following steps:

1. Refrain from language that either denigrates or inflates who you are as a person, in reaction to your circumstances. Do this by being objective about what happened: "I was laid off," "I won the award," "I was late to the party," "I lost my temper." Record what happened, and refrain from adding commentary "because I am a jerk"... "Because I am the smartest person ever." The more you can be objective and separate yourself from what happens, the more perspective you will be able to develop over time.

2. Remember that everyone wins some and everyone loses some. Humans have selective focus and often will select the times they have won and say "I'm a winner" or the times they've lost and say the contrary. Having confidence, taking risks and believing in one's self are great traits and get many people through the toughest of times, but painting your life with only one brush or another can be detrimental when things go against your belief system. Be confident, but be realistic and make sure you are taking the right steps to set yourself up for true success, instead of just believing you always come out on top no matter what.

3. Practice normalizing with a buddy. Having a friend join you on this journey can be helpful. Agree together you won't use all-encompassing terms such as "good girl" or "bad guy". Look at what you do well in any given situation, and what you might want to correct. Learning to give feedback to another person can help you with your own feedback. When you have a situation to consider, talk about what you did that you liked, and where you think you could improve. Consider what that improvement might be. What exactly could you do differently? What do you want to continue doing and reinforce? If you are new to this, having someone work with you on it can be very helpful.

4. Be careful of your self-talk. It's so common for people to use a circumstance as a springboard to that laundry list of all the things they love or hate about themselves. Catch yourself when you devolve into the

litany of how terrible (or how great) you are, and how you need to change yourself or stay exactly the same. Telling yourself you are all-powerful and can dictate the course of your life, for better or for worse, leaves you with too much power to make the wrong choice. Take the steps you need to take and be smart about them, but refrain from spending so much energy in your head telling yourself about yourself.

The story isn't always true, and you may find you actually limit your opportunities by doing this. Yes you have made mistakes in the past but that doesn't define who you are. You deserve to be loved, and appreciated. You deserve to be happy and to live life to the fullest. You deserve to enjoy intimacy and to be who you are. Be the best of you. Go out and soar like the eagle you are.

Change the negative perception you have about yourself.

How you see yourself in life is very important to your success in life. Your self-picture in face of challenges and storms of life, goes a long way to determine the outcome of the result you will get. Chuck Swindoll once said, "I am convinced that life is 10% what happens to me and 90% how I react to it."

It's easy sometimes to define ourselves by our circumstances, but I've found that this is a dangerous thing to do as there will always be things in life that don't go our way or that we don't control. If we attach our self-worth to the external, our sense of value can go up and down like a yo-yo. Defining ourselves by our circumstances also gives us too many excuses to remain in the place of pain that we've found ourselves in. We can repeat the same mistakes because that's how we see ourselves.

In Proverbs 23:7 (NKJ), the Bible says: For as he thinketh in his heart, so is he. This is a powerful statement that many are yet to come in terms with. I will not dare a cat that sees herself as a Lion. Let me share with you some examples in the bible were the power of self-worth and perception was put to a test.

Kick out the Grasshopper mentality

I recently finished reading Identity Crisis: Seeing Yourself as God Sees you by Frank Santora. It is a great book to readjust your image of yourself so that you have a Godly perspective. God created each of us with purpose, desire, and love in his heart. He made us to accomplish something, and He loves us deeply, but we walk around doubting, questioning, and failing to embrace these truths. This world speaks so many negative messages against us that leaves us feeling like we are insignificant and unimportant. Due to that, many of us will develop what I describes as the "Grasshopper mentality".

The grasshopper mentality is a phenomenon where a person accepts a pattern of thinking and behavior consistently below his/her true potential usually due to negative experiences in the past or a present challenge. Let me share with you a story that took place in the bible. If you read the book of (*Numbers 13: 1-33*), you will discover an amazing account of what best describe the power of perception.

It reads; Verse *1-2 And the Lord spoke to Moses, saying, "Send men to spy out the land of Canaan, which I am giving to the children of Israel; from each tribe of their fathers you shall send a man, everyone a leader among them."*

3-16. So Moses sent them from the Wilderness of Paran according to the command of the Lord, all of them men who were heads of the children of Israel. Now these were their names: from the tribe of Reuben, Shammua the son of Zaccur. From the tribe of Simeon, Shaphat the son of Hori. From the tribe of Judah, Caleb the son of Jephunneh. From the tribe of Issachar, Igal the son of Joseph. From the tribe of Ephraim, Hoshea the son of Nun. From the tribe of Benjamin, Palti the son of Raphu. From the tribe of Zebulun, Gaddiel the son of Sodi. From the tribe of Joseph, that is, from the tribe of Manasseh, Gaddi the son of Susi. From the tribe of Dan, Ammiel the son of Gemalli. From the tribe of Asher, Sethur the son of Michael. From the tribe of Naphtali, Nahbi the son of Vophsi. From the tribe of Gad, Geuel the son of Machi.

17-20. Then Moses sent them to spy out the land of Canaan, and said to them, "Go up this way into the South, and go up to the mountains and see what the land is like: whether the people who dwell in it are strong or weak, few or many. Whether the land they dwell in is good or bad, whether the cities they inhabit are like camps or strongholds. Whether the land is rich or poor; and whether there are forests there or not. Be of good courage. And bring some of the fruit of the land." Now the time was the season of the first ripe grapes.

21-25. So they went up and spied out the land from the Wilderness of Zin as far as Rehob, near the entrance of Hamath. And they went up through the South and came to Hebron; Ahiman, Sheshai, and Talmai, the descendants of Anak, were there. (Now Hebron was built seven years before Zoan in Egypt.). Then they came to the Valley of Eshcol, and there cut down a branch with one cluster of grapes; they carried it between two of them on a pole. They also brought some of the pomegranates and figs. The place was called the Valley of Eshcol, because of the cluster which the men of Israel cut down there. And they returned from spying out the land after forty days.

26-30. Now they departed and came back to Moses and Aaron and all the congregation of the children of Israel in the Wilderness of Paran, at Kadesh. They brought back word to them and to all the congregation, and showed them the fruit of the land. Then they told him, and said: "We went to the land where you sent us. It truly flows with milk and honey, and this is its fruit. Nevertheless, the people who dwell in the land are strong; the cities are fortified and very large; moreover we saw the descendants of Anak there. The Amalekites dwell in the land of the South; the Hittites, the Jebusites, and the Amorites dwell in the mountains; and the Canaanites dwell by the sea and along the banks of the Jordan."

30-33. Then Caleb quieted the people before Moses, and said, "Let us go up at once and take possession, for we are well able to overcome it. But the men who had gone up with him said, "We are not able to go up against the people, for they are stronger than we. And they gave the children of Israel a bad report of the land which they had spied out, saying, the land through which we have gone as spies is a land that devours its inhabitants, and all the people whom we saw in it are men of great stature. There we saw the giants (the descendants of Anak that came from the giants); and we were like grasshoppers in our own sight, and so we were in their sight.

Each time I read the above scriptures, I'm bewilder at the reports of these spies. I noted two points. Point number 1; these spies were all leaders of their respective tribes. Point number 2; they all had seen and experienced the wonder working power of God on their way from Egypt. In their very eyes, they saw God divides the red Sea, brought plaques to the Egyptians and rained down manna from heaven when they ran out on food.

This were the same people when faced with another challenge on their path, forgot their God, forgot His ability to protect them, forgot the miracles and testimonies of the past. They lost faith, and hope and resorted to negativity. They became so negative to the point of seeing themselves as Grasshoppers. Grasshoppers! Hmmm! big thumbs up to Joshua and Caleb, the two men who despite the fact that the challenge in front of them was big and fearful, they refused to be negative or hopeless. They had hope and faith. They remembered the victories and blessings of the past. They may not have physical power like that of the Sons of Anak, they may not have well-built muscles, or financial resources and military might like that of their adversaries, but they sure had the most powerful assert against any challenge; the power of self-worth and fearlessness.

Don't call me Naomi, call me Marah

Here is another examples from the bible that shows how challenges can cause a person to become so negative and even angry towards self. It's the story of Naomi the wife of Elimelech as recorded in the book of Ruth 2:1-21 (NK JV). Naomi and her husband and their sons Marlon and Chilion both migrated to the land of Moab for a greener pastures. When they arrived Moab, their two sons both got married to Moabite women, named Ruth and Oprah.

Years passed, and Elimelech, died and later on Marlon and Chilion both died leaving Naomi their mother alone with her two daughter in-laws. Frustrated and depressed, Naomi head of the economic growth in her country and decide to return home. As she approached the gate, her country women on seeing her shouted; is this Naomi? Don't call me Naomi she replied; call me Marah. The word Marah is the Hebrew word for bitterness. Naomi was indirectly saying to her country women that her name is no longer Naomi but bitterness.

Many people are in the same shoes as Naomi. They have change their name to something negative to reflect their anguish. Some have chased away friends and loved once because they don't want anyone to sympathies with them or tell them it shall be well. They have boxed themselves up, refusing help. They have withdrawn from entirely everything fun and exciting. They are dying slowly inside and they know it. Are you in a similar position in your life now? It's time to let go of the hurt and bitterness. It's time to move on and let the past be in the past. There is nothing you can do about the past and it events. Keep moving, keep living, everything is going to be fine with the passing of time. God is going to turn your mourning into joy and everything will work for your good.

Most people believe they are not extraordinary and they will never do anything special with their life. They don't want to get their hopes up because they have been disappointed so many times in the past. They don't aim for any goals in life because they are afraid of failure. It has often been said "If you don't aim for anything, you will probably get it."

It has been said that if you ask a person in any store why they are there, they will have a good answer, and they came to buy something or just came to look around. But if you ask a person why they are here in life and what their goals and dreams are, they will probably not be able to answer the question. Some say 8 out of 10 people don't really have an answer to that question.

A young man was told by his parents and teachers that he wasn't very smart. He didn't do well in school and after leaving high school he applied for a job at a large company near his home. The company always gave IQ tests to everyone who applied and they found that he had an extremely high IQ. They put him in a position that required a lot of thinking and planning. He did extremely well, in fact he invented a couple of new things and was awarded patents. What was the difference? He suddenly had hope and faith that he could do well at his job. He was treated with respect and it caused him to respect himself.

However, it is certainly true that many people who don't have much talent do incredible things in life. Many of the most successful businessmen, world leaders, inventors, athletes and rock stars do not have high IQ's. It is not necessary for success in life, by any definition of success. But it seems that hope is necessary and so is faith, or confidence, whatever you want to call it. Our self-perceptions are often instilled in us before we have a say in them. Learning to change how we see ourselves helps us find our hidden strengths, or improve weaknesses we didn't know we had, to get along better in life.

Accurate self-perception is a necessary component of self-improvement. If you don't know where your strengths or weaknesses lie, you don't know what areas you need to work on. Or how to leverage your assets! Self-perception is simply being aware of who you are, what you're like, and what you're capable of. Your self-perception goes beyond positive self-esteem, though. It may involve acknowledging your shortcomings ("I suck at playing the violin, and that's okay"), adjusting how you view your skills, ("This skill I thought was boring is actually useful and neat!"), or recognizing your problem areas ("I'm not as hard working as I like to think").

Adjusting your self-perception comes down to being honest with yourself. Recognizing your weak points helps you identify when you need to ask for help. Acknowledging your strengths can give you the courage to assert yourself even when you don't feel like you deserve to. What you do with the knowledge is a whole different can of worms, but here's how to adjust when your perception doesn't line up with your reality.

Prep Work: Identify Your Own Self-Image Fallacies

Often, we have self-perception problems because our emotions or misconceptions lead us to false conclusions. Anyone who's ever argued on the internet for more than a minute knows how easily logical fallacies can sneak in. When those leaps in logic face inward, though, they can alter how we perceive ourselves. For example: "I screwed up, so I am a screw up." This all-or-nothing mentality lends itself to low self-esteem, but it's a false correlation. We're good at dwelling on our mistakes, but bad at remembering when we got it right. The negative doesn't eliminate the positive.

"I'm not good at this yet, so I never will be." Everyone sucks at everything until they don't anymore. Failing a hundred times at something is discouraging, but it's incorrect to assume that those failures mean you're not good enough. In fact, those failures are how you get better. "Someone doesn't like me, so no one likes me." People who like or approve of us may not say it as often as someone with a grudge, so it's easier to focus on the negative.

"I've never had any complaints, so I must be good." Unfortunately, those closest to us may not always be the most objective reviewers of our talents. Until your skills have been put to the test in an arena free of bias (like the workplace or public performances), a lack of complaints doesn't prove talent. You'll probably never be completely free of internal logical fallacies. However, identifying when you're making a logical leap can kick start the process to learning the truth. From there, you can start making the necessary changes.

Step One: Perform a Self-Assessment

The first step in fixing your perception of yourself is to identify how you see yourself. One way to get started is a technique from cognitive behavioral therapy (or CBT) programs. Psych Central recommends writing ten of your strengths on one side of a paper, and ten weaknesses on the other. This exercise forces you to take an honest look at yourself:

This is your Self-Esteem Inventory. It lets you know all the things you already tell yourself about how much you suck, as well as showing you that there are just as many things you don't suck at. Some of the weaknesses you may also be able to change, if only you worked at them, one at a time, over the course of a month or even a year. Remember, nobody changes things overnight, so don't set an unrealistic expectation that you can change anything in just a week's time.

You may need to seek outside input from others if you can't come up with ten for both sides. Once you're done, keep the list because it will come in handy for the next thing you can do.

Step Two: Seek Outside Input (and Listen to It)

Outside input has the ability to either validate or negate how we perceive ourselves. If you think you're not that great of a singer, but the crowd at karaoke disagrees, you might start to change your opinion. For that reason, if you really want to adjust your self-perception, seeking outside input is absolutely necessary.

Author Scott H. Young offers some tips on how to get honest feedback. As it turns out, not everyone is completely forthright when you ask for an opinion (often for good reasons). Depending on the topic, you may need to coax out the full answer, or explain that it's okay to be honest: Read between Lines. Look for what they didn't say, not what they did. I'll admit this can take practice, but when you receive feedback where you question the sincerity, notice what wasn't said. If you wrote a how-to book, did they actually use the advice? If you gave a persuasive speech did they enjoy it or did it change their opinion?

Pull Out Gradual Honesty. Some people need encouragement to give you their honest opinion. Make it clear that you are okay with the harshest of their remarks and give them an opportunity to reveal more. Once you get feedback, listen to it. One of the most common mistakes we make when getting input from others is filtering out the stuff we don't like. I can totally play the guitar, they're just jealous, right? Nope. You asked for feedback, now accept it. If it's true, you'll probably hear it from more than one person. Be prepared to accept that the feedback you get is at least somewhat true, even if it's uncomfortable.

Step 3: Challenge Yourself and Step outside Your Comfort Zone

Of course, feedback from others is only one way to find out what you're capable of. There is a faster, more effective way, too: doing it. You may not think that you're good enough to get a job as an actor. However, nothing will prove you wrong faster than getting hired.

Of course, that doesn't mean that someone with asthma and high blood pressure should join the Army on nothing but a wish (unless your name is Steve Rogers). But having a realistic approach to what you can do, coupled with some optimism that things could work out alright, can be a key to making it happen. One psychological researcher named Sophia Chou at the National Taiwan University examined this concept of the realistic optimist. To put it simply, people who understood the risks but chose to be hopeful about the outcome not only performed better, but were happier:

Interestingly, the realistic optimists also got better grades, on average, than their less grounded peers — probably because they didn't delude themselves into thinking they would do well without studying or working hard, Chou said. Traditionally, a more realistic outlook is paired with poorer well-being and greater depression, yet the realistic optimists managed to be happy.

As Chou explains, people who evaluate their situation, but still challenge themselves anyway find that they're better equipped to handle those challenges. The result is a more successful outcome due to their preparation, but also an increase in satisfaction due to their moderate expectations.

Step 4: Emulate the Habits of Others

How you perceive yourself may affect how you behave, but the relationship also works in reverse. Simple gestures like faking powerful body language can help you feel more confident. This concept works fairly broadly. If you think you're too cynical, try being intentionally optimistic on social media. If you start deliberately hunting for the good in something, you may find it.

Our perceptions of our self and our relationships can be manipulated by things as simple as having a cell phone out at dinner. Putting the device away may make us feel as though we're more "in the moment" and strengthen the bonds we have with others. That means (somewhat ironically, in fact) that if your perception of yourself doesn't line up with reality, changing your external habits can influence how you perceive yourself.

It's weird enough that a phone on the next table at a restaurant might reduce the chances of two people hitting it off on a date. But the Swedish study points towards something weirder: not just that we're subconsciously influenced by our environments, but that we infer our very sense of who we are from our behavior. Normally, we assume things work the other way: that a person who thinks of herself as compassionate will therefore act compassionately. But "self-perception theory" proposes that the opposite's also true: we observe our behavior, then reach conclusions about who we are.

Our perceptions of ourselves will probably never be perfect (and a little self-delusion can sometimes help). However, many of us go years without fulfilling our potential or trying new things because we simply don't perceive ourselves as able. Or worse, we live with flaws because it never occurs to us that they're problematic. If you don't think you can go after your dream job, you're worried you can't attract that person you're really into, or you simply lack confidence, the problem might not be your situation, but just your perception. Your ideas about yourself determine the course of your life, so don't leave them to chance.

Chapter Twelve

PRACTICAL TOOLS FOR WALKING TALL IN TOUGH TIMES

Has life thrown you some tough times? Has there been a difficult situation in your past that you're still trying to recover from? Do you want to overcome all the stuff that's happening in your life and claim your happily-ever-after? Learning a simple formula for thriving in difficult times is everybody's wish. We all want to be able to surmount obstacles and move through life smoothly, without becoming intimidated by difficulties.

The ancient Greeks took pride in their practical approach to life: how they assessed situations, made decisions, and pursued complex goals; this gave them a unique power over storms of life. Life can be downright difficult at times. It can box you in and beat you down, holding no bars. While no one ever said that life would be easy, many of us were often ill-prepared for just how hard things could get. When we suffer through repeated failures and setbacks, getting through the tough times in life can seem like a fairytale fantasy.

How are we supposed to weather life's many storms? What happens when the burden of responsibility is just too great for any one person to bear? How are we supposed to get through the tough times, especially when we have little support from the people around us? Does it get any easier than this, or is this all we can ever really expect?

If you're going through a difficult time right now in your life, then my heart goes out to you. I sincerely feel for you because I've been there all-too often. I know the heartache and pain that comes along with major failure. I know what it feels like to have my life flipped upside down, not knowing where to turn or what to do next.

I won't insult you by claiming to know what you're going through, because when you're wading through the seas of hopelessness, that's the last thing you want to hear. What I will convey to you is the knowledge from my own personal experiences. I'll tell you how I made it through the tough times in my life using these practical tools and hopefully shedding some light on the subject and offering up a sliver of hope to you.

NUMBER 1: BE GRATEFUL FOR LIFE AND WHAT YOU HAVE

When life is good, feeling grateful is easy, but when disaster strikes, gratitude is worth the effort. Research on gratitude has shown that when life is going well, gratitude allows us to celebrate and magnify the goodness. But what about when life goes badly? During the economic maelstrom that has gripped our country, many wonder if people can or even should feel grateful under such dire circumstances.

My response is that not only will a grateful attitude help, it is essential. In fact, it is precisely under crisis conditions that we have the most to gain by a grateful perspective on life. In the face of demoralization, gratitude has the power to energize. In the face of brokenness, gratitude has the power to heal. In the face of despair, gratitude has the power to bring hope. In other words, gratitude can help us cope with hard times.

> *"Each day is a gift,*
>
> *Not a given right."*
>
> — *Nickel back*

Don't get me wrong. I am not suggesting that gratitude will come easily or naturally in a crisis. It's easy to feel grateful for the good things. No one "feels" grateful that he or she has lost a job or a home or good health or has taken a devastating hit on his or her retirement portfolio.

But it is vital to make a distinction between feeling grateful and being grateful. We don't have total control over our emotions. We cannot easily will ourselves to feel grateful, less depressed, or happy. Feelings follow from the way we look at the world, thoughts we have about the way things are, the way things should be, and the distance between these two points.

But being grateful is a choice, a prevailing attitude that endures and is relatively immune to the gains and losses that flow in and out of our lives. When disaster strikes, gratitude provides a perspective from which we can view life in its entirety and not be overwhelmed by temporary circumstances. Yes, this perspective is hard to achieve but research says it is worth the effort.

I know it's tough to look at what you have rather than what you don't have. It's partially a problem that's inherent in our society, one that has permeated our minds for ages. The truth? We usually want what we don't have, further worsening the problem. However, to get through the tough times, we need to look at our haves rather than our have-nots.

> *"Enjoy the little things, for one day you may look back*
>
> *And realize they were the big things."*
>
> — Robert Brault

Gratitude is the quickest pathway to happiness and peace of mind. Numerous studies have proven that when you're grateful, you're far happier. When you're trying to get through the tough times, you usually don't rely on your gratitude. Usually, you rely on your resentment, defaulting to your anger or upset, which is the quickest pathway to lead you further down the road of disappointment.

Do this every morning, spend at least 15 minutes writing out everything you must be grateful for. In the beginning, you'll find this difficult to do. But over time, as the habit builds, it gets easier. Keep in mind that habits take anywhere from 18 to 254 days to form, with an average formation period of 66 days. So, don't expect this habit to form quickly.

Every morning, find every little thing you can be grateful for. You can be grateful for the air that you breathe, the blood pumping through your veins, your limbs, your fingers, your mind, the fact that you can read, write and reason, the clothes on your back, the food on your plate, the fact that you're six feet above ground, and so on. Seek and you shall find things to be grateful for. Whatever you have, no matter how little it might be, even if they're problems, be grateful for them. Others around the world would love to have your problems, and problems are a sign of life. We will always have problems and we will always deal with times that can be extremely tough.

Trials and suffering can refine and deepen gratefulness if we allow them to show us not to take things for granted. Our national holiday of gratitude, Thanksgiving, was born and grew out of hard times. The first Thanksgiving took place after nearly half the pilgrims died from a rough winter and year. It became a national holiday in 1863 in the middle of the Civil War and was moved to its current date in the 1930s following the depression.

> *"There are only two ways to live your life.*
>
> *One is as though nothing is a miracle.*
>
> *The other is as though everything is a miracle."*
>
> *— Albert Einstein*

Why? Well, when times are good, people take prosperity for granted and begin to believe that they are invulnerable. In times of uncertainty, though, people realize how powerless they are to control their own destiny. If you begin to see that everything you have, everything you have counted on, may be taken away, it becomes much harder to take it for granted.

So, crisis can make us more grateful, but research says gratitude also helps us cope with crisis. Consciously cultivating an attitude of gratitude builds up a sort of psychological immune system that can cushion us when we fall. There is scientific evidence that grateful people are more resilient to stress, whether minor everyday hassles or major personal upheavals. The contrast between suffering and redemption serves as the basis for one of my tips for practicing gratitude: remember the bad.

It works this way: think of the worst times in your life, your sorrows, your losses, your sadness and then remember that here you are, able to remember them, that you made it through the worst times of your life, you got through the trauma, you got through the trial, you endured the temptation, you survived the bad relationship, you're making your way out of the dark. Remember the bad things, and then look to see where you are now.

Some years ago I visited a community in Legon Accra Ghana for a hospital outreach, and when I entered one of the rooms in the male ward, I met a young man whom I guessed was around my age, with a pipe and a bottle hanging down his waist. I asked one of the nurses around why he had them on and the nurse told me that he was experiencing serious pain peeing through his penis, so they had to connect that pipe into him, so he could pee through it.

Just as I was talking with the nurse, this young man cried out in pains as he was peeing right before my very eyes. It was if the Holy Spirit was teaching me a lesson about gratitude that day. As soon I came out of the hospital I had the urge to go and pee. While peeing, my mind went back to that encounter inside the ward, the excruciating pains that young man was experiencing while peeing.

I looked down and saw my pee flowing like a waterfall, with ease and not even the slightest discomfort, and I cried out loud. I knelt and thanked God for the privilege to pee freely. Nothing is more important than health, but we take these things for granted only to realize their importance when sickness or accidents hit us.

> *"Be thankful for what you have;*
>
> *You'll end up having more."*
>
> — *Oprah Winfrey*

In this crazy world of material things and endless seeking for more, most of us forget to take time to be grateful for what we do already have. Tony Robbins once said "Success without fulfillment is the ultimate failure". Developing an attitude of gratitude is essential to a fulfilled life and therefore a successful life. The truth is gratitude has a compound effect in your life. The more you practice being grateful, the more reasons to be grateful for will show up. When you get grateful for what you have now, you will soon have more to be grateful for and it's so true. When you send out those feelings of gratitude, what happens is you become instantaneously happy, in that moment.

When you are grateful and happy with life, as it stands today, so many more things will flow into your life to be happy and grateful for. And the reverse is also true: if you feel like there is nothing to be grateful for, what are you focused on? You're focused on everything you don't want, you are focused on everything you don't have, and what do you then think you will attract into your experience? Exactly, more of what you don't want.

"Some people grumble that roses have thorns;

I am grateful that thorns have roses."

— Jean-Baptiste Alphonse Karr

Make it your mission to sit down every day and get grateful. Get grateful for those two gifts you have called eyes, many aren't so lucky. Get grateful for the ears that can hear music. Get grateful for that person in your life that made a difference. Be grateful that you can make a difference in someone else's life. Get grateful for your tough times, because they helped develop your strength and spirit. Get grateful for your life. I am grateful for life, for my family every day. There is so much to be grateful for.

There's something to be said about being appreciative and grateful. Whether you're thanking God, or life, or whether you're looking to a person in your world and just saying thank you, there's something special about that. I mean, there's something very real about moments where you can just sit by yourself, and look at your life, and just say thank you. You know, thank you for this gift. Thank you for this ride that I'm on, thank you for this journey.

And a lot of people go through their lives without experiencing the beauty of these moments. Your life, although perhaps filled with many imperfections, is still an experience. It's an experience that people in their final moments would do anything just to grasp onto for a little while longer. As you read this book, they are taking their final breaths. Taking their final breaths on this planet. Looking back at their lives and wishing they could have done more.

> *"Gratitude is the key to*
>
> *Ultimate riches."*
>
> — *Joel Osteen*

Meanwhile, we have this experience, we are alive, we're breathing air, our hearts are pumping, and our brains are doing billions of operations per second, just to keep the game going for us. We can't find reasons to be grateful for that? You can't, as a human being, be appreciative for that? There's an entire spectrum of life you are missing out on when you don't take moments to just feel. Just feel!

Just create moments of gratitude within yourself, just for the sake of being appreciative. For the sake of being alive. That alone will change your life. That will make you human again. That will disconnect you from this game of consumerism and this dog-eat-dog world we've allegedly created. That will disconnect you from the insanity of society and reconnect you with something greater than yourself.

When you begin to be appreciative for life, there is a certain power that will bring you even more reasons to be appreciative. It's one of life's greatest paradoxes. When you are in a state of needing this and needing that, it doesn't matter how much you acquire, you will never have enough. But, when you have the courage to be grateful for what you already have, life will bless you with even more. You know, you can decide, in this moment, to give it up. Give up the complaining; give up the blaming and the accusing. Give up the gossiping and the whining and instead, realize you are on an incredible journey and fall in love with every second of it. That's when you will truly come to life.

NUMBER 2: ACCEPT AND EMBRACE THE SITUATION

Sometimes you're an observer of other people's lives and you think you'll never experience what they're living, whether it's a positive or negative situation. You think, "That will never happen to me." Part of the real beauty of life is that it's unpredictable. Nothing is permanent, everything changes; and of course, a lot of things can happen that will transform who you are and have an impact on your life. The problem is that we need to cultivate the ability to truly accept whatever comes and embrace it. We need to develop the habit of looking at whatever happens through a positive mindset instead of a negative, defeatist one.

> *"Reality doesn't bite, rather*
>
> *Our perception of reality bites."*
>
> — *Anthony J. D'Angelo*

Of course, life will bring many challenges, and it's not easy to embrace them when we're suffering and wishing those things would have never happened. But if we start cultivating acceptance in our lives right now, we'll likely cope with future crises in a different way and view them from a different perspective. We will accept instead of resisting.

I am a big fan of Deepak's Chopra's book: *The 7 Laws of Spiritual Success*. He dedicates one complete chapter (law #4) to how we need to receive with open arms what happens to us, because if we fight and resist it, we are generating a lot of turbulence in our minds. He explains that we might want things to be different in the future, but in the present moment we need to accept things as they are. That's the way you can make your life flow smoothly instead of roughly. There are two ways out of a problem: accept what's happening, see the positive, and choose a peaceful state of mind; or fight against it, be miserable, and struggle against the universe.

Acceptance, in my opinion, is the key to convert momentary happiness to enduring happiness. It helps you move from feeling happy to actually being happy. Practicing acceptance prepares you to live in this changing world, where you never know what's going to happen next. Acceptance is like protecting yourself with your own shield. Let me clarify that acceptance is not at all related to weakness and is not a synonym of conformity or mediocrity. We need to learn how to identify when it's time to persist and when it's time to accept. One thing that makes acceptance much easier is to list all the possible explanations for why you're experiencing something.

Finding the lesson or purpose behind every challenge will help you embrace it instead of fighting it. Choose not to judge what happens to you. Instead, believe that everything happens for a reason and that better things will always follow. That's the beginning of true acceptance. Somewhere recently I read that the important thing is not to understand why something happened. Our understanding can wait, but our obedience cannot. I translate this to mean that when something unpredictable happens, instead of complaining and overthinking it, we need to choose to live with it.

> *"Any problem embraced is half won*
>
> *Already because it has lost its*
>
> *Power to keep you down."*
>
> *— Serena Williams*

I know it's hard to practice acceptance when you deeply wish things were different. But the truth is, sometimes we can't change our reality, even if we try. So instead of staring at the closed door in front of us or getting tired and bruised while we try to break it down, let's turn around and see how many other windows we have open. No matter how chaotic things are, they do not define you. Your past does not define you. You are defined by what you think about yourself.

NUMBER 3: CHANGE YOUR PERCEPTION

I'm a big believer that some of the most important, worthwhile lessons in life are often the simplest, the most overlooked. One of my greatest realizations is that any situation is far less important than your interpretation of it. In fact, I go as far as to say that anything in life is simply a product of the meaning that we give it.

As Wayne Dyer said, "If you change the way you look at things the things you look at change." And this is extremely significant because it unblocks any door in the world. To be able to have that perspective, that understanding, that you are the one in control. Knowing that will undoubtedly take you places. The question of course is what you are doing about it. It's no secret that if you look at things with a negative lens they're going to appear negative.

If you look at life as this giant tragedy in which you're always the helpless victim, guess what? You will remain that way. You're essentially enabling a self-fulfilling prophecy. We are who we believe we are. The world around us exists as we allow ourselves to see it. Words like difficult, impossible, they have no meaning. They don't even exist until we give them life. Think about it. We are creating negativity, you know, constructing barriers that have absolutely no reason to be up.

I like to simplify this equation, because to me it's about having a goal and achieving it. That's it. If you're at point A and you want to get to point B then there are really two options: you can map out your path and make it happen or you can create reasons why it's not possible, reasons why you can't do it and success isn't for you.

By starting with the little things, like waking up early or changing eating habits, we look at what's in front of us and we ask why, we don't ask why not. And here's my take: if human beings got a man on the moon you can come up with a strategy to wake up early without hitting the snooze button. It is that simple and this applies all the way up the ladder to larger things like running the marathon, getting the promotion, on and on and on.

Kick out the Grasshopper Mentality

Let me share with you a story from the Bible, which to me is the greatest book on earth. This story clearly illustrates the power of perception during negativity or challenging situations in life.

If you are a Christian and you study the Bible, you would have heard or read about the story of the twelve spies Moses sent to scout out the land of Canaan as recorded in Numbers 13:1 - 15:41. When Moses sent these scouts to survey the land of Canaan, he gave them a list of very specific things to investigate. He charged them: *"Go up through the Negev and on into the hill country. See what the land is like and whether the people who live there are strong or weak, few or many. What kind of land do they live in? Is it good or bad? What kind of towns do they live in? Are they un-walled or fortified? How is the soil? Is it fertile or poor? Are there trees in it or not?"* (13:17-20, NIV). Twelve emissaries went out and returned after forty days, reporting on what they saw in this exotic new land.

"Miracles happen every day,

Change your perception of what a miracle

Is and you'll see them all around you."

— *Jovi Bon Jovi*

Each of the men Moses sent to carry out this secret espionage were leaders from their respective tribes. They had all been under the same leadership of Moses. They all had experienced the power and love of God toward them from Egypt, how He divided the Red Sea for them to cross, how He made manna rain from the sky. Yet despite all these miracles, when a challenge arose, 98% of them became intimidated, afraid, and reduced.

To show the extent of their fear, and their perspective of the circumstance, they went ahead to call themselves *"grasshoppers"* in the eyes of the men they encountered. Now with such a defeated mindset and perspective towards the situation, defeat is unavoidable. But thank God for Joshua and Caleb, the two men who had a different perception of the problem. They saw victory, and they refused to be intimidated or feel reduced. They told the entire congregation of Israel that they were capable of overcoming.

See yourself as someone who wins, who succeeds. Leave all that other baggage behind you, it helps no one. They say some of life's greatest accomplishments were achieved by people who didn't know they were once considered "impossible". They had a target and they hit it. Before you even think about your specifics you have to know that a solution is out there, that it exists, it's just a matter of whether you will make it happen. That's where it's so important to set yourself up to succeed, to brush the negativity aside and to analyze what's in front of you with the lens of someone who can and will get the job done. When it comes to being resilient, the ability to reframe is an essential skill.

> *"The difference between average*
>
> *People and achieving people is their*
>
> *Perception of and response to failure."*
>
> — **John Maxwell**

Reframing is the ability to look at a situation or circumstance in a new way, giving it a more positive or insightful spin. "At the simplest level, it's changing perspectives, changing the way you look at something, or trying to understand whatever you're seeing or involved in. I've been seeing this one way; let me change to a different way of thinking about it," says Lee G. Bolman, a Brookline, Massachusetts-based scholar, consultant, and author of the recently released book titled: *How Great Leaders Think: The Art of Reframing.*

Surround yourself with positive people. Quit associating with things that tell you anything but yes. Life is hard enough as it is. You don't need additional hurdles. It's about you and that goal. You and your objectives. Not can you, but how will you. When you change the way you see the world, when your intentions are positive and powerful, when you search only for the good, then your life transforms into the amazing adventure it was designed to be. After all, anything and everything in life is all up to interpretation. In other words, there is no such thing as reality: you create your own reality with the thoughts you think.

NUMBER 4: BE CONSISTENT, DON'T GIVE IN

You will never be truly great unless you are consistent, in everything you do. Success is not a one time, or short-period thing. It's an every single day thing. Sometimes it takes 10 years to get to that one year that will change your life… just keep going. Remain consistent. Consistent in your work ethic, consistent in what you stand for, consistently showing up every single day, rain, hail or shine. When everything is great, and when nothing is. Keep showing up!

You said you tried? And it didn't work. You said you did everything. You read the books. You put in the work. And it still didn't work. When did anyone say it only took one try, two, five, ten tries? When did any successful person mention that you only need to give your best effort for one month, then you'll be successful? When did any great person mention they only gave their all for 6 months or any period? When did anyone say giving up will get you closer to your goal?

I'll tell you when: never! Do you think you only need to give your best for a year and then you can live the rest of your life successful? Think again! If you want to make your dream your reality you have to be consistent; that's every single day! It never ends! It never ends! It's every single day. When you feel like it, when you don't, when you're getting results or when you're not. When someone is watching, when they're not. When they believe in you, when they don't. When you believe in yourself. When you don't. When it seems possible, when it all appears impossible.

If you want a great body: it's every day. If you want to improve your finances: it's every day. If you want a great life: it's every day. Every day learning, every day putting in the hours, every day working harder than yesterday. Every day believing it's going to come! Every day, consistent! Even when it seems there's no hope in hell! You believe, one day you'll be in heaven on this earth! The quote doesn't say, we become what we do sometimes. The quote doesn't say we become what we do when we feel like it. The quote doesn't say we become what we do for a short time, before we eventually give up. The quote says: we become what we do consistently!

I become what I do consistently! And you can also say, you will become what you do and what you believe. Consistency is the key to success in life. In the gym, in your growth, in your finances, in your relationships, consistency is essential. Sometimes it takes 10 years to get to that one year that will change your life, just keep going.

"One thing guys have to remember

Is consistency...you can't make up for three years

Of eating poorly in just one workout."

— *Apolo Ohno*

Remember Why You Started

When you feel like quitting, remember why you started. When you feel like quitting, don't. Push through the pain and get your reward. When you feel like quitting, remember all of those who said you'd fail. When you feel like giving up, remember why you started.

When you feel like quitting, remember what you're doing it all for. When you feel like quitting, remember pain is temporary but greatness lasts forever. When you feel like quitting, remember that the pain you feel today will be replaced with the strength you need tomorrow. Remember that every ounce of pain you feel is building a stronger you, a stronger body, a stronger mind, and a stronger character. So, push through the pain and don't let it stop you, rather force it to grow you.

Don't back down from the pain. Face it! Too tired: yet no excuses! Too hard: yet no excuses! Too busy: no excuses! Too early but no excuses! Too stressed: no excuses! When I feel like quitting, I remember: there are too many people I need to prove wrong. When I feel like quitting, I remember: I have too much to fight for! I will not quit.

Your greatest physique, your greatest health, your greatest strength, they don't come with average effort. If you want average results, keep rocking up and giving average effort. If you want to be at your best, you will have to give your best effort.

Make an oath to yourself that you will not walk out of any training session, any game, any battle you are in now, anything, without giving 110% of your soul. It could be your marriage which is about to crash, it could be a rebellious child, don't give in to defeat. Fight until you rescue your marriage, your relationship. Whatever you think is your limit, push past it.

Whatever you think is your max, see if you can get 10% more out. Results don't lie. It all comes down to one simple question: how bad do you want it? Nothing great is going to come if you quit. I know it's hard. I know you are tired. I know it seems impossible, but you must keep going. Stick it out and get your reward.

Shut Out the Distractions

If you want to achieve high level results, you must shut out all meaningless distractions. If you want to reach your goal, you must shut out everything that interferes with your goal. In today's world of over stimulation, seemingly unlimited distractions, and short attention spans, it's no wonder there are so many people who don't succeed. It's no wonder so many people never achieve anything significant. It's no wonder so many people never reach their true potential. If you want to achieve anything great you must shut out all distractions.

Successful people are focused people. They can go into a space where they shut out everything. Where they lock in on the task in front of them. Lock in on their goal. Lock in on their dream. A recent study pointed out that the average adult spends around 1 hour and 40 minutes every day on social media! That is nearly 12 hours per week! Over 50 hours per month, 616 hours per year. It adds up to 128 days over a period of 5 years. 128 days wasted every 5 years.

Imagine if you used that time better. Imagine if you replaced that wasted time with completely focused time, working on something you love. The person you will be in 5 years' time will be very different depending on which path you choose to take.

Those who don't succeed, let's call them the majority. They are like a puppy with a bone. Anytime a bone comes along… social media likes or comments… a text message… a TV show… an opportunity at another night out… any attention or meaningless distraction, they drop everything important to them, and chase bone. They could be sitting on a million-dollar idea, something that could change their life completely, but as soon as that bone comes along they follow it. Day in day out. Meaningless distractions tearing people away from a life they deserve.

Meanwhile they are left feeling empty inside because they haven't fed their soul with the pride that comes from self-growth. Growth from shutting out the world and going all in on their dream. Growth from finding a way when there seems no way. Growth that comes when you go beyond the life you thought you were capable of.

> *"When everything seems to be going against you,*
>
> *Remember that the airplane takes off*
>
> *Against the wind, not with it."*
>
> *— Henry Ford*

Every time you choose something over your goal, you form a bad habit, a habit that gets stronger and eventually overpowers your goal. It defeats your dream. Form a different habit. A habit of discipline. Discipline from shutting out what most won't so you have the things most don't. A habit of going all in. A habit of integrity. When you say your goal matters to you, show that it matters! Make it a priority! If you want to achieve great things, shut out the distractions of this world and make your goal a priority.

Steve Jobs once said, "People think focus means saying yes to the thing you've got to focus on… but that's not what it means at all. It means saying no to the hundred other good ideas that there are. You must pick carefully. I'm actually as proud of the things we haven't done as the things I have done." You must be able to shut out everything but the most important thing that you must do right now. Get it done with 100% of your presence and attention. Give it everything you have, your heart and your soul. That will ensure your best work and will lead to your next best result.

Zig Ziglar said, "Lack of direction, not lack of time, is the problem. We all have twenty-four hour days." Now, that's the truth, if I have ever heard it! We all have 24 hours in a day. How you spend that time will determine where you end up in life. How you spend your 24 hours will determine if you live with pride or regret. How you spend your 24 hours will determine if you survive or you thrive. Now it's time to focus! Lock out the things you don't need. Lock in on the life you must have! Prepare to suffer now so you can enjoy later.

NUMBER 5: UNDERSTAND THE POWER OF ATTITUDE

There is nothing as powerful as attitude. Attitude dictates your response to the present and determines the quality of your future. You are your attitude, and your attitude is you. If you do not control your attitude, it will control you. Attitude creates your world and designs your destiny. It determines your success or failure in any venture in life. More opportunities have been lost, withheld, and forfeited because of attitude than from any other cause. Attitude is a more powerful distinction in life than beauty, power, title, or social status. It is more important than wealth and it can keep one poor. It is the servant that can open the doors of life or close the gates of possibility. It can make beauty ugly and plainness attractive. The distinguishing factor between a leader and a follower is attitude.

What is attitude? It is simply defined as "the mindset or mental conditioning that determines our interpretation of and response to our environments." It's our way of thinking. It is also important to understand that attitude is a natural product of the integration of our self-worth, self-concepts, self-esteem, and sense of value or significance. Your attitude is the manifestation of who you think you are. Leaders think differently about themselves, and this distinguishes them from followers.

The story of the lion and the sheep demonstrates the power of attitude. We live our attitudes and our attitudes create our lives. The difference between the attitudes of a lion and a sheep determines their place in the scheme of the animal kingdom. Perhaps that is why the creator, as recorded in the books of the Hebrew writer Moses and other biblical writers, identifies Himself with the unique temperaments or natures of certain animals.

We live our lives based on who we think we are. If you believe in your heart that you are a sheep, then you will stay in the confines that others have placed you in or that you have made for yourself. If you think that you are a lion, then you will venture beyond manmade limitations and embark on the life of leadership that you were born to live. You will develop into someone who inspires and influences others within your inherent domain no matter the conditions surrounding you.

No amount of training in leadership skills, courses in management methods, power titles, promotions, or associations can substitute for the right attitudes. I am convinced that all the money in the world may make you rich, but it can never make you a leader. Your leadership development is determined by your perception of who you are and why you exist. In other words, your sense of significance to life.

Every day, life brings new opportunities and presents you with thousands of new choices. One of the first choices you get to make each day is about your attitude. Yes, whether you realize it or not, attitude is a choice. You can't just wait and allow your circumstances to dictate your attitude; you must be on the offensive and choose your perspective for each day. When you wake up with enthusiasm and choose to be grateful, you are "putting on" the right attitude. You are setting your day up for success and opening the door to be used by God in a powerful way.

Everyone faces difficulties. We all have obstacles that can seem impossible to overcome. However, the difference between those who can rise above their adversities and those who get stuck in them is attitude. There's an old saying, "attitude determines altitude." In other words, a positive, faith-filled attitude will cause you to rise higher in life, but a negative, self-defeated attitude will only drag you down.

When we face adversity, our attitude affects the outcome. Are we going to treat people right even when we're being mistreated? Are we going to stay full of joy even when the bottom falls out? So many people get all bent out of shape and start complaining when things don't go their way, but that kind of attitude only closes the door to God's miracle-working power. The Bible says that faith is what pleases God. Understand that He's trying to work in your life. He's trying to get you prepared for promotion, but you've got to stay on His side. You've got to stand strong and fight that good fight of faith!

If you are going through a difficult time today, keep an attitude of faith and expectancy. Start thanking God for bringing you through to the other side. As you stand strong, you'll rise higher. You'll come out stronger and wiser, and you will experience the abundant life God has for you!

> *"The picture that we have of ourselves — our self-concept —*
>
> *Will always determine how we*
>
> *Respond to life."*
>
> *— Myles Munroe*

A thankful attitude is a form of praise. It shows that your faith and hope are in Almighty God. I believe it is one of the main keys to living the abundant life God has in store! Today, you may have some negative things happening. You may have some challenges or unexpected situations crossing your path, but remember, a thankful attitude and a heart of praise will empower you to rise above any adversity! The Bible says; *"Enter his gates with thanksgiving and his courts with praise; give thanks to him and praise his name."* (Psalm 100:4, NIV).

The scriptures admonish us in 1 Corinthians 10:13 (NIV), *"No temptation has overtaken you except what is common to mankind. And God is faithful; he will not let you be tempted beyond what you can bear. But when you are tempted, he will also provide a way out so that you can endure it."* Some of the challenges we face in life may be very difficult ones, but God never allows more to come upon us than we can bear. In fact, with every temptation, He always provides a way out. The scripture above not only says He provides a way out, but it also says He gives us the strength to bear up under trials with patience. That means we can go through them with a good attitude! Maintaining a good attitude during something unpleasant is the key to victory, and it enables us to enjoy the journey.

The Nature and Attitude of the Lion

"Leadership can transform Cowards into violent warriors."

— *Myles Munroe*

There are two animals on the planet that the Creator identifies Himself with. The first one is the eagle and the second is the lion. And when I discovered that these two animals are His favorites to identify Himself with, I went and did a lot of study and research about these two animals. And I discovered that both animals are the kings of their domain.

The eagle is the king of the avian (bird) kingdom, and the lion is the king of the wild animal kingdom. But let me share with you more about the lion. You see, the lion has what I call the spirit of leadership, and this word "spirit" here is referring to attitude. A leader has an attitude that makes him or her different from followers.

Now the lion is the king of the jungle, but the lion to me is a great source of encouragement to all of us. I want you to note this and always remember this forever:

- The lion is not the tallest animal in the jungle
- The lion is not the largest animal in the jungle
- The lion is not the heaviest animal in the jungle
- The lion is not the smartest or the most intelligent animal in the jungle
- The lion is not the fastest animal in the jungle

But when the lion shows up every animal runs away. Why is the lion running the forest with all these limitations? This is just to tell you that, you don't need all these things or any kind of advantage to be a leader. You have no excuse not to become a leader. It is your mind that makes you a leader or a follower. Your thinking should stretch above the limitations of the norm. Attitude is a product of belief. You cannot have an attitude above your belief. Your attitude comes from your belief system. The lion believes he is the king and so he is.

You see an army of sheep led by a lion, will always defeat an army of lions led by a sheep. And the explanation to this dilemma is this: Leadership can transform cowards into violent warriors. The right kind of leadership can transform a group of timid people into bold people who are fearless. Leadership is that powerful.

Leadership can walk into a camp of depressed people, and in less than 30 minutes they are turned into unbelievable, powerful armies. Because leadership determines everything. The lion is the king of the jungle because of one word. "Attitude". The lion has a different attitude that makes every animal afraid of him in the jungle. Now I am not saying you should lead by fear, but it does take respect for you to become a leader. When I use the world "fear" in the jungle I'm talking about respect.

"An army of sheep led by a lion,

Will always defeat an army of lions led by a sheep."

— Myles Munroe

The elephant respects the lion. The hyenas respect the lion. The giraffes respect the lion. Now the question that got me thinking is this: what makes these massive animals respect such a small cat? The attitude is the difference. For example, a lion will see an elephant and the thing that comes to his mind is one word: "lunch". I can eat this thing. And he goes ahead and acts the way he thinks.

And here is another amazing mystery: the elephant is larger, bigger, stronger, more powerful, heavier and more intelligent and yet when the elephant sees the lion, one word comes into his mind: "eater". You see, attitude is a product of belief and you cannot have an attitude beyond your belief. So, your attitude comes from your belief system. The lion is the king because of what he believes about himself and he has successfully passed this mindset and attitude to his young cubs from generation to generation.

I am a great fan of the National Geographic Wild channel and many times I have watched how the lioness takes time to teach her young cub the art of hunting and tearing of flesh into pieces. That is why no matter the size of the lion, its instinct and sense of dominion and control is still intact. The other day I watched on National Geography S as this tiny cub was chasing a very big deer. And I was amazed at the courage, boldness and survival instinct.

This is how we ought to think, act and talk during trials and storms of life. Not to complain, cry, withdraw, or feel frustrated, defeated and helpless. No, rather face your obstacles with an overcomers' attitude and mindset. See the victory in your mind's eye. I think sometimes it's good for you to take out time and study some of these animals; you will be amazed at the level of adaptability they show when their surrounding changes, or whenever danger approaches.

Develop the strength and definiteness of a lion! Develop the lion attitude. The attitude that says I can, the attitude that says I will. Sheep follow the leader. They follow the herd. They don't know where they are going. Many times they are led to the slaughter house! But they keep following! They don't lead! They don't use their mind!

> *"The same boiling water that softens potatoes,*
>
> *Also Hardens eggs. It's all about what you are made of*
>
> *And not your circumstance."*
>
> —*Joyce Meyer*

A lion leads! It's about having the courage to stand and fight for your life. Having the strength to go bravely in your own direction! Even if others walk away, you tread your own path! Only you know what's best for you. Only you know what path to take. Only you know your courage, your strength, your heart. Everyone has the heart of the lion inside them! Let it out! Let it scream out of you. Unleash the lion in you!

Attitude is what you think, what you do and what you feel about yourself. Attitude is everything in life. Guess why? Whether you rise or fall — everything is based on the attitude you showed at that moment. Your attitude will determine your altitude. I've been through tough times. I've experienced it and I want you to know it wasn't my money that brought me this far, it was my attitude towards life. It was my decision to keep going when the going got tough. That is the lion attitude I am talking about. The question is, what is your attitude towards life?

What do you think of yourself as you read me now? Do you think of yourself the way God thinks of you? Or do you think of yourself the way friends and family members think of you? You need the lion attitude. The attitude to take charge of your destiny. You need the lion attitude that says "I can", you need the lion attitude that says "I will", because I am bold enough to fight! You need the lion attitude if you are aiming for greatness!

Real lions, they are hungry when the time comes for their mission. Lions are not followers! They are leaders who lead the rest of the animals.

Become a lion! Be fearless! Don't talk. Walk the talk. Real lions demonstrate who they are. A lion does not seek respect. They command respect and authority because they know they should be respected. Be a lion! A sheep follows the leader. A lion leads! It's about having the courage to stand and fight for your life, having the strength to go in your own direction! Even if no one believes in you!

> *"Victory and defeat*
>
> *Begin from the mind."*
>
> *— Bishop Harry Jackson*

Follow your heart! Only you know what's best for you. Only you know what path to take. You have the heart of the lion inside you! Let it out! Don't fit in! Stand out! And use your gift! The lion is certain. There are no maybes with the lion: "This is my decision and I will attack until the outcome is mine! No one will push me around! No one will tell me where to go or what to do! If I want something I will go after it with everything I have inside me!"

The sheep is not certain! That is why the sheep follows the herd. Not knowing where they are going. Not caring. Just drifting through life. Being pulled and prodded. Being sheared from head to toe until there is nothing left to give! And that is what I see in many. Life, the world, and society is shredding you of your very self. Head to toe you lose your own unique footprint! You become what others want to see, not what you want to be! Don't let anyone push you around! Be like the lion! Roar so loud with your own spirit that no one will doubt you ever again! No one will question your goals! No one will dare challenge you again! Because your certainty will shine through! Like the lion.

NUMBER 6: SEEK OPPORTUNITIES TO CONTRIBUTE SOMETHING TO OTHERS IN NEED

One great way to make it through the tough times in life is to contribute something to someone else. You don't need to donate money, but you do need to donate your time. What can you do to help someone else? This is a great way to shift your focus. When you contribute to others, you're also sending a very powerful signal to your subconscious mind.

> "We make a living by what we get;
>
> We make a life by what we give."
>
> — *Winston Churchill*

There is a Chinese saying that goes: "If you want happiness for an hour, take a nap. If you want happiness for a day, go fishing. If you want happiness for a year, inherit a fortune. If you want happiness for a lifetime, help somebody."

For centuries, the greatest thinkers have suggested the same thing: happiness is found in helping others. The starting point for all happiness is shifting the focus away from yourself. If all you think about is yourself, you're going to be a pretty miserable person. If you truly want to be happy in life, you must care about the needs of those around you.

When you give your time or donate something else to others, you're telling your mind that you have more than enough. Even if you don't consciously think that, the signal that's transmuted is precisely this. And when that thought permeates your mind, it helps to give you a sense of gratitude. Not only do you realize that others might be far worse off than yourself, but you feel good about what you're doing.

One thing that I realized over the years is that life is about contribution. While humans might govern themselves, physically, on the selfish-survival principle, that's not how many of us live our lives. We give to others, donating our knowledge and our expertise, finding the time to help people who can't help themselves. Simply put, there's just no better feeling than this.

> *"The sole meaning of life*
>
> *Is to serve humanity."*
>
> — **Leo Tolstoy**

So, put some serious thought into this. Grab a sheet of paper and ask yourself what you can do for others. What value can you contribute to the world? How can you help people that are in need? Again, this isn't about money; this is about your time, which is far more valuable in my opinion than any amount of money because time can't be regained; once it's lost, it's lost. Going through a hard time? Then help others who are struggling. It may seem counterintuitive to reach out to others in need when you're feeling so needy yourself. But when you help other people, you help yourself, too. Helping others is a healthy habit to develop, no matter what circumstances you may be going through. While your focus is on blessing other people, you'll find that God blesses you in a wide variety of ways.

NUMBER 7: REDISCOVER YOUR SELF

Many times when crises hit we tend to forget our self, our values, our purpose, our strength and even the things that bring us joy. Sometimes we lose sight of ourselves. It happens to the best of us. Even the most successful and self-aware people can go through phases where everything seems… off, somehow. But it doesn't have to stay that way. In fact, getting lost can be an awesome opportunity to rediscover and redefine ourselves, perhaps uncovering an even more fulfilling version of ourselves that has been trying to push its way through.

Still, that process of discovery is a process. And so, like any process, there are strategies you can employ to help you move through it.

What is Your Why?

Finding your reason why, your purpose, is essential if you want to achieve success. If you don't have a strong reason behind your actions, your actions are less likely to create quality results. If you do have a strong "why" you have all the fuel you need to drive you forward to success. What is your why?

When you wake up every morning — what drives you? If you want to live a life of success, a life of complete success, happiness and fulfilment, you must find your purpose. You see, if you don't know what your purpose is, if you don't know what drives you, what inspires you, then you have no reason to improve your life. How can you improve your life if you have no reason to improve it?

Why do you do what you do? What's the reason? Why do you exist? Do you know what it takes to be great? Are you willing to go the extra mile? I tell you, time and time again you will get tired. But if you have a why, it will give you that extra strength. That extra foot you need. That extra hour you need. The courage. Why are you different from everyone else that's trying to do the same thing you're doing? What makes you stand out? Why are you so important!?

Your why will pull you up when you feel like you don't have the strength to get up anymore. Your why will keep you fighting when everyone else thinks you are out for the count. Why? Who are you fighting for? What drives you? Is your purpose your family? Is it to prove the doubters wrong? Is it to prove yourself right? What is your purpose? Write down your purpose. Carry it with you everywhere. Feel it deep and promise yourself every day you will live out your purpose with zero excuses!

Somebody's waiting for you to mess up. Somebody is waiting for you to give up. Someone is waiting for you to fall. So, when you are challenged by life, what are you going to do? When you feel like you are at your lowest point in life, will you throw in the towel? Or will you make the moves to be successful? Don't look back. Just remember where you came from. And let that drive push you to go forward. It's not always going to be an easy road, and when you reach success, you won't take it for granted. You will cherish those moments you had to go through, those moments you were without. And when you fall, get back up. Dust yourself off.

You need to find something that drives you. Something that, no matter what happens, this part of you does not change. This drive in you does not change. This purpose never dies. No matter how many times life knocks you down, your purpose pulls you up every time.

"This is the reason I will fight for my dreams!"

"This is the reason I will not take no for an answer!"

"This is the reason I will do whatever it takes!"

When it hurts keep going. Those cloudy days, those storms, they're telling you to keep going.

There will be those times in your life when you can't see how you're going to make it. Some things you can't change, you just must live with. But if you do have a choice, make the right choice. Your purpose is that one thing that lights you up. It's that one thing that will get you up early. That one thing, when you're doing it, time stops. Your purpose may be something you don't want. It may be seeing someone in your past and thinking: no matter what, I will ensure I never end up like that.

Your purpose is always something that lights a fire in you. "I will do this. No matter what. My family is counting on me! My friends are counting on me! I am counting on me!

The Lone Wolf

It's not easy going it alone, but keep going and the right people will show up in your life.

If you keep going, stay true to yourself… it will be worth it in the end. The hardest walk you can make is the walk you make alone, but that is the walk that makes you the strongest. That is the walk that builds your character the most. To you fighting battles alone. To all of you going against the grain, battling the naysayers: stay strong! Keep going!

This walk is hard. But the hardest walks lead to the greatest destinations. The toughest climbs always lead to the best views! It will be worth it in the end. And if you show what you are made of, the right people will show up in your life. You won't be a lone wolf forever. You have qualities only few can admire, because most don't possess. You have strength only few can understand, because most have never experienced.

So, don't give in, don't settle, and don't lower your expectations to fit into the world. You were born to stand out. You were born to lead. Lead the pack. They say the wolf on the hill is never as hungry as the wolf climbing the hill. Always be that wolf, climbing the hill, always hungry for more! Always hungry to grow, to feed your mind, and to rise to the highest level you can take yourself. Never looking back, always looking forward, to the next feast. Feast of success, in whatever you do. It doesn't matter if you must walk alone for a while. It is much better to walk alone in the right direction, than to follow the herd walking in the wrong direction.

NUMBER 8: CONFESS THE WORD OF GOD AND THINK POSITIVELY

Now to me as a believer, this is very important, because the Word of God is the surest weapon against anything on earth. When you are passing through difficult times, remember what the word of God says about you. Confess the word over your life.

The word of God says you are victorious, you're a royal priesthood, and you're a holy nation, a chosen generation, the apple of His eyes, and His ambassador on earth. So, despite what you might have experienced or are experiencing, that does not define you. Yes, you are divorced, but that is not who you are. Confess and declare the word over your life. Say, I am blessed, I am different, I am born again, I am the light of the world, my better days are here, my time is right, I am free from sin, sickness, sorrow, grief and fear, I do not want, Jesus is made unto me wisdom, righteousness, sanctification and redemption.

As you consistently confess these words over your life and circumstances, you're gradually purging yourself from negative thoughts, depression, regrets, self-pity and any form of the enemy's hold on you. This may sound crazy, but it is as powerful as anything. The word works. I have applied it and seen it work for me.

Think from the basis of the word of God and not from the basis of the circumstance surrounding you. God knows what you're going through, and He will never allow you to be consumed by it. He said in Jeremiah 1:5 (NIV); *"Before I formed you in the womb I knew you, before you were born I set you apart; I appointed you as a prophet to the nations."*

He also made it clear in Jeremiah 29:11, *"For I know the thoughts that I think toward you, says the lord, thoughts of peace and not of evil, to give you a future and a hope."* This is the promise of God to you.

He said His thoughts and plans towards you are of good and peace. That means whatever you are going through right now, if only you will believe His word, they are all going to work for your own good.

See what He promised you in Isaiah 43:2 (NIV) *"When you pass through the waters, I will be with you; and when you pass through the rivers, they will not sweep over you. When you walk through the fire, you will not be burned; the flames will not set you ablaze."* Wow, what a promise. This is the word I take very seriously. I held God by it when I lost my father, and when I suffered from a serious respiratory tract disorder that was threatening my life. He said He will not let the circumstance consume me. He said He is with me always. Now if God be with me in the valley, why do I need to fear about the shadow of death?

> *"I would rather be with the Lord in the valley,*
>
> *Than stay alone in a mansion without God."*
>
> — **Great Igwe**

I know you might say, "Great, how do you know God will keep His promises?" Oh yes I know because He said so in Matthew 24:25, *"Heaven and earth shall pass away, but my words shall not pass away."* So, the question is not if God will do it, the question is "are you going to believe His word?" Use this word as your tool, confess it daily. When the enemy tries to steal your joy, chase him out with this word. Eat the word, bathe with it and let it saturate your subconscious mind daily.

Why Positive Confession Matters

Words have power. They can hurt, and they can bless. But the power of words reaches much further than the impact they make on our emotions. Our words have supernatural power that changes circumstances and shapes destinies. In fact, it is our unique ability to choose and speak words that distinguishes man from the rest of God's creation.

Man is created in God's image and it was not just thoughts but words that God used to create us and the universe in which we live. When He said, "light be," light was. Words are the way God works. Hebrews 11:3 (KJV) describes this operating principle of creation this way: *"Through faith we understand that the worlds were framed by the word of God, so that things which are seen were not made of things which do appear."*

Words are spiritual; they carry power. Proverbs 12:14 tells us that we shall be satisfied with good by the fruit of our mouths.

This process begins with salvation. The lost man does this when he declares Jesus lord of his life: *"The word is nigh thee, even in thy mouth, and in thy heart: that is, the word of faith, which we preach; that if thou shalt confess with thy mouth the lord Jesus, and shalt believe in thine heart that god hath raised him from the dead, thou shalt be saved. For with the heart man believeth unto righteousness; and with the mouth confession is made unto salvation."* (Romans 10:8-10, KJV).

Confession is not denying physical facts and temporary circumstances. It is declaring what God, who never changes, has said about the outcome and standing in faith until all temporary conditions line up with His eternal declaration.

Confession is a vital part of our spiritual growth as believers. Jesus indicated this in describing the importance of speaking His Father's words and not His own: *"I do nothing of myself; but as my Father hath taught me, I speak these things...If ye continue in my word, then are ye my disciples indeed."* (John 8:28, 31, KJV)

In answering the question of how He would manifest Himself to His disciples after His resurrection, Jesus replied: *"If a man loves me, he will keep my words: and my Father will love him, and we will come unto him, and make our abode with him. ...the word which ye hear is not mine, but the Father's which sent me"* (John 14:23-24).

Israel's King David understood this. He brought his soul (his mind, will and emotions) in line with God's word by speaking to it: "Bless the LORD, O my soul, and all that is within me, bless His holy name. Bless the LORD, O my soul, and forget not all his benefits." (Psalm 103:1-2, KJV) Confession of the word of God isn't lying. We are not trying to get God to do anything. Those benefits GOD has given us in His word are ours already and Satan is trying to steal them!

The process of believing and speaking is what brings every benefit of our salvation promised in God's word from heaven into our lives. To tell someone you are healed because the Bible says "by His stripes you were healed" is speaking the truth. Jesus has already redeemed you from the curse of the law (Deuteronomy 28, Galatians 3:13).

Words reveal what we truly believe. Jesus said, *"Out of the abundance of the heart the mouth speaketh...By thy words thou shalt be justified, and by thy words thou shalt be condemned."* (Matthew 12:34, 37, KJV). That is why it is so important to say what God has said. Do this not so others can hear you, but so your soul will receive instruction as to what to believe and agree with instead of the symptoms in your body, situations in your life, and fear-based thinking and talking you hear from others around you.

"Positive thinking will let you do

Everything better than negative thinking will."

— Zig Ziglar

How do we give glory to God? By honoring the words He has spoken and demonstrating our trust in Him. Our first step of acting on our faith in His word is to agree with and say the thing He has said.

Keeping Jesus' words means more than just doing what He said. It also means living as He lived. He lived never saying or doing anything He did not first hear the Father say or see the Father do. As His disciples, our words should be in complete agreement with what the Father has spoken concerning us. When we speak His words in faith, they have the same power to change our circumstances as when He spoke creation into being.

Jesus' ministry to us today includes His position as high priest of our profession, or confession (Hebrews 3:1). To profess means to "say the same thing." When we say only what God has said, His words have the same power spoken in faith out of our lips as they did when He originally spoke them. Jesus, as our high priest, makes sure those words the Father has spoken come to pass in our lives. That is why we are instructed to "hold fast the profession [confession] of our faith without wavering; (for he is faithful that promised)." (Hebrews 10:23, KJV). See also Hebrews 4:14.

If you are not a believer in Jesus as the only way to God the Father, the truth and the life, I pray that this book ministers to your spirit about this man called Jesus. But, whatever you believe in (Allah, Buddha, or the spiritual oneness that binds us all), learn to rely on your faith and remember that this too shall pass. Tough times don't last, tough people do. But to become a tough person, we often need to rely on something far greater than ourselves. This isn't solely about religion. If you're not a religious person, rely on your spirituality.

We are all interconnected in this universe. Every atom and cell in our body has come from a single source at the beginning of time. Whatever you believe in, you must believe that there is invisible ether that runs through the fabric of life. Just because we can't see it, doesn't mean that it isn't there. For me, it's all about God and my belief in Him.

> *"Keep your face to the sunshine*
>
> *And you cannot see a shadow."*
>
> — *Helen Keller*

Whenever we open ourselves up, spiritually or religiously, we're inviting in an element to our lives that doesn't exist when we're closed off or simply living a material existence. It's one of the most powerful feelings that you can experience in your life when you allow yourself to just live and be present. There is a purpose and a reason why you're going through the tough times, you just don't know it yet.

NUMBER 9: KEEP THE RIGHT ASSOCIATIONS

One of the important tools for walking tall through tough times is the support of good friends and family. With the right kind of folks around you, there is no mountain you cannot climb because these people will encourage you, support you, and strengthen you with kindness and love. My father used to say that when one man is chasing a lizard alone in his house at night it might seem too big, as though it's a giant snake, but with the help of the neighbors the lizard will always be like a lizard.

The kind of friends you hang out with will matter when trials arise. Remember that true friends are not created in times of success, but rather true friends are created in times of storms. People have a huge impact on your life. "You are the average of the five people you spend the most time with," says American entrepreneur and motivational speaker Jim Rohn. You should think about the people you're spending time with the same way you think about what you eat and how you're exercising.

There are certain kinds of friends you will have, and no matter what you are experiencing they are always there with you, encouraging you, motivating you and giving you hope. They will see the ocean facing you and say "Man, you can cross it, I know you. You are strong, you are brave, and you are smart." With such words entering your ears, your mind begins to tilt towards such thoughts and you begin to see yourself doing the things you ordinarily wouldn't be able to do. These are the kinds of associations you should surround yourself with.

On the other hand, there are those friends who are happy when you fall into the pit. They use your situation as a public discussion. Instead of supporting and encouraging you, they are even praying you never come back. And don't blame some of them; they are that way because of inferiority complex. They know you are far better than they are, and so the only way they can feel good about themselves, is to see you suffer and fail.

Let me share with you a story about the power of supportive friends in our lives. Amanda was battling with blood cancer. The doctor told her she had only 6 months to live, as nothing could be done. Amanda had given up on herself, but Jorine and Neola, who had been friends with Amanda for nine years, refused to give up on her. Every morning, these two ladies would rush to Amanda's house and speak words of encouragement, telling her stories of many people who went through similar conditions and made it.

They continue to pray with Amanda, comfort her and take her out almost every day just to make her forget her situation. As if that was not enough, they arranged for a vacation with Amanda to Singapore and while there, they engaged her in all manner of fun events and comedy, dances and beach parties, which made her so happy that she almost forgot she was sick. Two weeks after they came back she went to the doctor for her checkup and the doctor told her that from the current diagnosis, she had an 89% chance of fighting off the cancer. This made her so happy and lively again. Amanda died in August 2014 but she lived for seven extra years before she died. All because her friends supported her, and never gave up on her.

Some people can be parasites. They suck out your happiness, energy and maybe some of your tangible resources as well. You can put spending time with them in the same category as eating nachos on the couch. When you hang out with the right people, yes darkness will come, but your friends can help make your darkness comfortable and worth enduring.

When you are up in life your friends get to know who you are. When you are down in life you get to know who your friends are. There will be many people who will be great to be around when times are easy. Instead take note of the people who remain in your life when times are hard. The friends that are willing to sacrifice their time and the resources they have in their life to help improve yours. Those are your real friends. A real friend is one who walks in when the rest of the world walks out. I like you to bear in mind that not all that laugh and smile in your face, actually mean well for you. And not everybody who calls you brother or friend is your friend. Some are wolfs in ship clothing. This is why you have to be wise in your selection of friends.

When the world turns against you, when darkness suddenly takes over your light and when your world seems to be crumbling down, that one friend will look you in the eye, hold your hands and say: I've got you, let's go through it together. Those are the kinds of friends you need, and their support and presence is very necessary in the season you are in.

But if you have no friends, then walk through it alone, or build relationships.

These moments are crucial in life because it's when you realize who matters and who doesn't. Only true friends will stick by you through tough times, help you in every way they can, and are always there to listen to you. Life is fragile. Hard times are inevitable. At one time or another, we will all go through a difficult time, whether we deal with sickness, catastrophe, crisis, or relational breakdown. In those times, we need each other more than ever, but it's not just enough to be surrounded by people. We, as supporters, need to be educated on the best ways to love our friends and family through tough times.

NUMBER 10: LEARN FROM IT AND DO THE THINGS THAT GIVE YOU JOY

When I find myself in middle of an ugly situation, I like to pick everything apart and see what went wrong and what I could've done differently. I always end up learning something that helps me and I eventually get a clear picture of what I need to do to make sure I'm not in the same situation again. Or if I do find myself in a similar situation, I know what to do to minimize the difficulty of the situation.

It's easier getting through a difficult time when you know the chances of it happening again are slim to none.

"Nothing ever goes away until it

Has taught us what we need to know."

— Pema Chödrön

When we fail, or something doesn't work as expected, we begin realizing and investigating what went wrong. We learn and identify our mistakes. If we're lucky, we hear constructive criticism, feedback that enables us to identify our weaknesses or skills that need improvement. It's crucial to recognize, identify and acknowledge the problems. If we had not failed, we would not have found those weaknesses in the first place, let alone fix those.

As we identify our mistakes and weaknesses, we learn unusual and unique lessons. We gain a greater understanding of people and how they respond to various situations. We learn diversity and practical aspects that contribute to success or failure. The experiences we learn from failures are often more interesting than the joy of success itself. Difficult times also push us out of our comfort zone.

We feel we are in a constrained environment and that leads us to be creative and think out of the box. We feel challenged to perform higher than before and within constraints. This encourages us to become extra mindful regarding resources, matters we have been taking for granted otherwise. When we feel challenged, we work and attempt beyond the traditional approaches and often this results in something impressive and unimagined. Difficult times guide us to understand not only our drawbacks, but also our true potential and abilities.

If we were not challenged or not put in a constrained environment, we would not have performed to our greatest potential. We learn to seek out our countless other skills and abilities. All the previous failures and difficulties that we endure makes us further confident and adequately prepared for future challenges.

We become experienced at risk taking, planning for unforeseen events and trying the latest adventures. All those experiences urge us to strive for even newer challenges and adventures. Those difficult times, all the unusual experiences and learning we gained, transform us into a stronger, smarter person than before. We grow more experienced, with further lessons learned and higher risk appetites. All this learning allows us to contest even bigger, even larger adventures that we didn't explore yet.

I have discovered that if I engage in activities and hobbies that I love when I am experiencing hard times, it always lifts my spirits. When we do what we love, it grabs our attention and focuses it away from whatever is making us unhappy. My loves are cooking, writing, swimming and watching cartoons. You will have your own favorites and it is extremely useful to tap into them. Think of it as a form of meditation and mindfulness. Now these activities won't make the problem disappear, but they will surely help you daily to thrive.

Do something that makes you happy. What makes you happy? Pull out a sheet of paper and write it down, right now. Don't wait until later. Brainstorm 10 things that fill you with joy and elation. Maybe it's spending time with your kids, maybe it's driving up the coast, maybe it's reading a good book, maybe chatting with friends, whatever it is, write it down. Next, go about doing one thing that makes you happy every single day. Schedule the time for it like you would schedule the time for a meeting. Devote at least 30 minutes to it. If you love eating cookie dough ice cream while watching your favorite guilty pleasure on television, then write it down. Whatever it is, be sure to jot it down and devote the time to it. While this won't help solve your immediate problems, it will give you some momentary relief during the toughest of times in life.

Rise and Face Your Goliath

As I bring you to the end of this book, I want to encourage you to rise and face your Goliath. Your relevance, your promotion, all lies behind your big giants now. Usually our first response to adversity is to run from it. We need to run toward it instead. Every invitation to greatness is accompanied by obstacles and mountains that must be faced. Adversity is nothing more than an incubator to process the destiny of men and women who are going to change the course of history.

> "Sometimes God will put a Goliath
> In your life, for you to discover
> The David within you."
>
> — *Bishop Harry Jackson Jr*

Push

You see, the journey to greatness is like childbirth. If you are a woman you will understand what I'm saying. When a woman goes into labor and enters the delivery room, they call it the labor room. In the labor room, there is no makeup; there is no Brazilian hair, no Louis Vuitton bags, no Victoria Secrets, no expensive diamonds. No, the labor room will mess up all of that.

> "When life gives you lemons, make lemonade."
>
> — *Proverbial phrase.*

The labor room is the room of the birthing of a new vision, a new purpose, a new idea, a new identity and a new personality. It won't come easy, blood will flow, your water bag will burst, sometimes you might get some cuts, and sometimes it will just be you alone in the labor room. You might scream out so loud, experience a lot of excruciating pain, but you've got to push. It is coming out, but you must keep pushing. This is your destiny, this is your life, and you must push it out. And just as it is for the mother, when the baby comes out, it will all be worth it. The pain, the rejections, the cuts, will all be worth it.

> *"If size mattered,*
>
> *The elephant would be king of the jungle."*
>
> — *Rickson Gracie*

Many times, the very problems we think are going to destroy us become the platform for our promotion. We don't like to admit it, but we need enemies in our lives. The enemies we face make us aware of areas of need in our lives that we would never have recognized had we not faced the enemy. Some of the greatest discoveries in my own life have come because of adversaries who sought my demise. And who knows if we would have heard of David had there not been a Goliath, or of Moses had there not been a pharaoh.

Your friends create comfort, but your adversaries bring creative movement. It is not until we get tired of being harassed or taunted that we rise with decisive action to begin the process of maturity and growth. Creativity, boundaries, strategies all are born when a "giant" appears in our pathway. Our willingness to respond releases God's power on our behalf.

I know what it is to fight giants that have come to hinder my progress and try to force me into boundaries of limitation and isolation. Comfort zones are no protection against giants. Neither is running from the giant. If you don't run toward the giant and overcome it, you will find yourself running into a life of make-believe success and significance. Before long, you will find that your success and significance are nothing more than tattered, worn-out "tents".

> "God doesn't give the hardest battles to His toughest soldiers, he creates the toughest soldiers Through life's hardest battles."
>
> — *Bishop Harry Jackson*

Don't cower in timidity from the mocking voices of your Goliaths — run at them instead. But never run at them with your mouth shut! That is a formula for defeat. Declare His name, Jesus! The mention of His name causes the forces of hell to tremble. With his simple slingshot and a mouth full of confidence, David ran toward Goliath. With one release of the stone, the giant fell. David ran and cut off Goliath's head for the king. A great victory had been won! God does not want you to live in the shadow of your Goliaths, fearful of the future. Afraid to step out or speak up. Instead, He wants you to face your Goliaths. Live in victory... Free to experience all His blessings and live out the faith He offers you.

The story of David and Goliath can teach us much about how to face our giants in this life (even when the biggest Goliath in your life is you!). Friends, if you are always weeping over criticism and rejection, continually frustrated because somebody misunderstood you, or upset because some group of friends won't let you in their group anymore, you must make the choice to break free today! Your progress and future potential demand it. Don't allow the voices of a few to rob you of His voice saying, "well done!"

The Struggle Makes You Stronger

Struggles, challenges and hard times offer you much more value than any other time in your life. You cannot grow without struggle. You cannot get stronger without resistance. Think about a time in your life that may have been hard but forced you to become better. Get grateful for the struggles and work on yourself to ensure your future has much more pleasure than pain.

Imagine if you got what you wanted, every time. No struggle. No challenges. No hard work required. Some of you are saying that would be great. No, you would be weak! And then, when something hard comes up in your life, you wouldn't know how to handle it, because you have never gone through anything that strengthens you. You cannot grow without struggle. You cannot develop strength without resistance, without challenging yourself.

Pain is your friend. Maybe not in the moment. But for the evolution of your soul, for the long-term benefit of you as a stronger human being, pain is your friend. If you didn't have failures, if you didn't have struggles, if you didn't have disappointment, you could have no strength, no courage, and no compassion. How could you? Those qualities are made from your pain and struggle. You were given pain because you are strong enough to handle it. You were given this life because you are strong enough to live it. Because you are strong enough to drive through it, to thrive through it. To inspire others through it. They will look to you and say: he did it, she did it, and I have the strength to do it too.

"Never be ashamed of a scar,

It simply means you were stronger

Than whatever tried to hurt you."

— Dwayne Johnson

You are stronger than you think. You've survived all your challenges to this point and you will survive whatever is coming. But next time a struggle comes I don't want you to curse the skies. Know that it was sent for a reason and a lesson. It might be to make you stronger, it might be to teach you patience, it might be for you to show others your spirit; there is a reason.

So, don't you give up! You have a purpose in this world. And you will only find it if you keep going and keep growing.

It's Never Too Late

Many people fail to go after what they want in life because they think their best days are behind them. It's never too late to create your best life. No matter what age you are, no matter how many past failures, it is never too late.

It's never too late because success is all in the mind. You can define success however you like, so if you can control your mind you can create your best life. If it is financial or material success you are seeking, it is never too late for that either. You are only a Google click away from a world full of "late" success stories. Some of the greatest, most successful humans on the planet only made it big later in life. Never give up, you are capable of anything you can imagine.

There is no greater pain than that of regret. Nothing can kill your soul more than the feeling of regret. Never be afraid to take a risk in life. Never be afraid to take a risk going after what you really want. You may fail, you will most likely fail often. But failure going after your dreams is nothing compared to the failure that is settling for a life you don't want.

It's never too late to try again! It's never too late to decide you want more out of life. It's never too late! It's never too late to commit to make this day, this very day, the best of your life! To create opportunities for yourself. To be positive. To rise above average thoughts. It's never too late to re-invent yourself. To learn something new. To grow, to feel good again. No matter what has happened or failed to happen in your past; it is never too late. But only if you are committed. Only if you want to change.

Do you want to change? Do you want more out of life? You wouldn't be the first person on earth to turn everything around. It is not impossible.

All it takes is your commitment, your courage and your desire to be better. Most people don't change because they lack courage. Because they fear the unknown. They fear failure. You are different. You have the courage, the courage to try. Don't fear failure. Fear being in the exact same place next year as you are today. Nobody is going to make your dream a reality! That's up to you. That's why you can't give up. This is your dream!

And you are capable! You are more than capable! Never settle. Never settle for less than you're worth! If you are suffering. If you are fighting through pain, through adversity, whatever you are going through: do not give up! It will get better! After the rain comes the rainbow. After the storm the sun will shine. Even on the cloudiest days, your sun is still shining. Just wait for those clouds to pass. Tomorrow is a new day, a better day.

It's time! Today is the day! The first day of the rest of your life! Make that commitment. Show me your courage! Be fearless! Never give up. Can you hear me? Even if you're living in your car. Even if you're sleeping on the side of a gas station. Never give up! You've got to keep fighting. Because if you stop, nobody's going to pick you up. Those cars are going to continue to roll past you. But you keep walking!

It's that destination that you have in your soul. It's where you want to make it. See, your tears will become the ocean that leads to your paradise. Whether you're a man, a woman or a child, the toughest battles come to the toughest warriors. You've got to see it like it's already in your hand. You've got to walk like you're already a star. Even if you have nothing in your pocket. That pride, that purpose, that gift will give you the ability to walk into the room, full of millionaires, and they all will want to know you. But you can never give up.

You can never stop fighting for that top spot. See, you've got to become rich on the inside, before you can become rich on the outside. You need this. So, when you get to the top, you know how it feels to be at the bottom. You know how it feels to give another person a shot. Never give up! Make good choices today so you have no regrets tomorrow! Be brave today so you have no regrets tomorrow! Live fully today so you have no regrets tomorrow. No more regrets! No turning back! I'm all in! All in for my goals! All in for my dreams! Make your pain pay you.

Dry Bones Are Becoming Flesh

There is a God who has the power to turn dry bones into flesh. It's not about how dry the bones are. If you will only believe, I tell you, these bones will become as flesh. In Ezekiel 37: 1-13 the Spirit of the Lord came upon the prophet Ezekiel and took him to a valley filled with dry bones. And the Lord asked Ezekiel a very profound question, "Son of man, can these bones live?" And Ezekiel said, "You alone know." The Lord instructed Ezekiel to prophesy to the bones and while he was prophesying, there was a rustling, a noise, a movement amongst the dry bones.

Suddenly, the limbs were coming together. Suddenly, the tendons, the cartilage and all the tissues were coming together. And behold, the entire valley of bones became an army of warriors, a people of praise. And the Lord spoke to Ezekiel saying, "These bones are the whole house of Israel."

These bones represented their challenges, their relationships, their marriages, their finances, their businesses, and their health. They had become desolate and dried. But now God was arising among them, bringing flesh on their dry bones.

All they had lost, all that had happened to them, all their discomfort and pains, their rejections, betrayals, abandonment and everything that had stolen their joy, God was now turning to their advantage.

See what the Lord said in Ezekiel 37: 11-13 (NIV);

Then he said to me: "Son of man, these bones are the people of Israel. They say, 'our bones are dried up and our hope is gone; we are cut off.' Therefore prophesy and say to them: 'this is what the Sovereign LORD says: My people, I am going to open your graves and bring you up from them; I will bring you back to the land of Israel. Then you, my people, will know that I am the lord, when I open your graves and bring you up from them.'"

Whatever you are experiencing, or whatever you've lost, the Lord is saying He is bringing restoration and double for your shame and troubles. He is opening new opportunities, new ideas, new streams of income, new friendships; He is sending your way someone who will love and appreciate you for who you are. All those who have laughed you to scorn, condemned you, mocked you, and criticized you, they are about to see a new you; they will come to you for forgiveness and become jealous of the blessings coming your way. There is a shift coming your way. Kiss your cares goodbye for there is a new transition, a crossing over to a place of creativity, a place of dominion, because you have been pushed by a supernatural force.

**ptbbp*Your Scar can birth a Star*

Every tough battles that comes our way, will definitely leave a scar on us. Be it emotional, physical, spiritual, mental or financial battles, they will always be a form of scars that will remind you of what you have gone through, the battle you have fought, the pain you have endured and very importantly the loss and emptiness. This scars should not limit you, don't be shy about it, and rather be proud of it, why? Because it announce your strength, you're never give up attitude, your resilience, patience, and your courage. Not everybody can go through what you have gone through and still be as strong and full of energy as you are. Not everyone can withstand and endure the pains and hardship you have experienced and still rise above mediocrity and average existence.

Not everyone can experience the rejection and betrayal you have experienced in life and yet be full of love and compassion in there heart for others for it takes courage to love and pour out yourself into another. They are so many successful men and women whose Scars became the defining moment of their life and pave the way to their greatness and success in their life. Some it took them by surprise while others strategically turn their Scars to a star.

There is no champion without a scar. These Scars are not necessarily physical injuries on your skin although to some that may just be it. When you go into a jewelry store, and you see a gold or diamond jewelry starring at you, all you notice is the beauty of the Jewelry, the glamour and perfection of it. But before that beauty and elegance, was hours, days and months of being crushed, mixed, put into fire and beaten hard.

The subjection of these precious metal to such pain and toughness is a process that the mineral needs to go through in other for it to become the beauty you admire in the store. Some years ago, I visited a zoo in Botswana in Africa and I had the privilege of being taken around the park were the Chimpanzees lived. There was a particular chimpanzee by name Jegede that got my attention.

Jegede was brought into this Zoo from Ethiopia after a wildfire destroyed her previous habitat. When this chimp was brought in, the other Chimps already living in this Zoo, did not want her to be a part of the family. For months Jegede has to fight his way through to relevance among the group. While the Zoo keeper took me around, I could not help but notice Jegede because of the scars all over his body. When I ask the Zoo why the scars on Jegede? He told me that the mark shows what Jegede has gone through to become the leader of the group. He said Jegede was never welcomed to the group when he first came into the Zoo, his fellow Chimps never wanted him around them.

Jegede was living like an outcast among his fellow chimpanzees. When food is brought in, they gang up against him so he won't eat from the share, they prevented him from mating with any female chimpanzees in the ranks.

These went on for some months and one day Jegede began to fight his way through to get food and to mate with the females. As these went on for a long while, with each day beginning and ending with a fight for survival, fight to feed, fight for space, for mating, and above all fight for recognition. This fight always left a scar on Jegede body. It came to the point where Jegede became a chimp not to be messed around with. He goes for what he wants and gets it. No chimpanzee dare stands on his way.

He became so prominent and powerful and soon became the leader of the group. Jegede story made him stands out when visitors visited the park. Every visitor to the Zoo, rushed to his section just to behold these chimp who has fought and gone through hell to become relevant and powerful among his fellow chimps. The Zoo management even had an article about these particular chimpanzee Jegede.

Friend, let your scar be your story. Let it inspires others, to see that with a determination and a heart of a fighter they can win any battle. Let your story motivate others not to give up. How often we go through life, picking up scars along the way. We get battered down by circumstances and, sometimes, we even get battered down by other people. Many of us try to hide those scars, to mask them, and to pretend they were never there to begin with; however, scars never truly go away, do they? There really isn't some special cream we can rub on our hurts, our fears, our insecurities and all of the other scars we collect throughout life.

There isn't any magic elixir that will remove the scars we carry with us. Even Jesus, in a post-Resurrection body, had scars to show his disciples when he appeared to them. The holes in his hands, feet and side were still there, still visible. In fact, those scars were very much a part of Jesus' transformed identity. Friend, rather than trying to erase the scars, rather than trying to bury them or hide them or pretend they never existed, you should acknowledge their existence. It okay to grieve the loss, the hurt, the circumstances that caused them and, just as importantly, you should also acknowledge the person you've grown to be as a result of them. While no amount of reflection will justify the suffering we've been through, it will help us to move beyond the suffering, remembering where we've come from, and resurrect into a person transformed by the grace of God in spite of the experiences that tried to keep us down. Allow God to, as Robert Schuler once coined, "turn your scars into stars."

I Hear the Sound of Abundance of Rain

I don't know what your situation is now, I don't even know who you are, but I want to speak to you as a servant of the living God: I hear the sound of the abundance of rain coming your way. In 1 Kings 18:41 (NIV), the Bible says; *And Elijah said to Ahab, "Go, eat and drink, for there is the sound of a heavy rain."* Did you hear that? What does that rain signify? Rain represents harvest, growth, newness, cleansing, and above all rain represents blessings. So, cheer up, for I hear the sound of an abundance of rain coming your way.

You're about to get wet. The rain is about to overtake you. God is going to rain upon you His blessings that you won't be able to hold. So rise, raise your umbrella for your dry season is coming to an end. Gird your loins; the blessing, the job, the car, the house, the healing and the relationship are about to set in. All your wasted years are about to produce manifold blessings. Everything that the locust, the cankerworm, the caterpillar, and the palmerworm have eaten off you — it might be your health, your job, your marriage, your business, your contract, your house or your family — God is restoring all back to you.

Are you going to believe His word?

Notes

Notes

Notes

Notes

Notes

www.ingramcontent.com/pod-product-compliance
Lightning Source LLC
Chambersburg PA
CBHW030313080526
44584CB00012B/553